★ RAVING REVIEWS ★

This book is emotionally engaging, practical, and utterly relatable. As a fellow entrepreneur, I tend to read a lot of self-help that glorifies the meteoric rise of individuals that find their 7-figure success but gloss over a LOT of the emotional struggles and steps required to be a sustainable and long-term success as an entrepreneur.

Prit's story and self-leadership are at times heartbreaking and inspiring as she delves into the all-to-real struggles of what it's like to be a broke entrepreneur, when things don't always go right, and how to find your purpose and passion when your life just isn't going to plan.

I highly recommend this book as it's not only a solid read; it's just such a testimony to the amount of growth Prit's had to go on to find her purpose and passion. If you're a struggling entrepreneur, or someone even remotely interested, this book will give you hope when it feels like none exists and remind you why you were inspired to be an entrepreneur in the first place.

Ken Reid | Counsellor | @ken.reid.co

Zero to Four Figures is a must-read for any digital entrepreneur. Prithvi Madhukar shakes up the industry by redefining success and encouraging readers to believe in themselves, celebrate every achievement, and embrace the journey.

Through engaging storytelling, Prithvi sheds the veil, sharing personal anecdotes, hard-learned lessons, and invaluable professional insight perfect for new entrepreneurs. As a digital nomad and business owner, I found the lessons pertinent, relatable, and actionable.

Zero to Four Figures is the best medicine for burnout. You will reach the end feeling reinvigorated and inspired.

Michael Camarillo | Author of Keeper 829 |
Founder of Novel Excursion | www.novelexcursion.com |
@michaelcamarillobooks

Prit's book is a gallon of entrepreneurship, a lifetime's worth of lessons, and the things that get in our way. She brings in magic from the business experiences that taught her and the life experiences that made her. You'll laugh, you'll cry, and you'll learn to be proud of yourself. That's Prithvi Madhukar's first book for you!

Meghana Sridhar | Freelance Copywriter |
linkedin.com/in/ meghana-sridhar

This book will help and encourage many solo digital entrepreneurs who are mainly struggling all alone. You'll recognize yourself in the words and be encouraged that you are not alone, that someone else went through what you're going through and came out good.

You'll also learn strategies you can try with the corresponding workbooks to assist with implementing those strategies. I learned quite a bit myself. It would be pointless to single out any part of the book as the best because all the chapters speak to an entrepreneur.

Folasade Taiwo | Money Mindset Coach | @financialsavviness

The whole part felt like it was written by someone who is a friend! I never thought I was reading a book! It was like my very close friend was narrating the lesson of their life, that too very poetically! Enjoyed every tad bit of it!

Jaskirat Singh | Co-Founder—Brand Monkey Marketing Agency | www.brandmonkey.in

Prithvi Madhukar has taken a daunting subject such as being an entrepreneur and presented it in a way that everyone can read and enjoy. Whether you're just starting your business, or it's been something you've been going at for a while, the material presented in the book can be useful.

Prithvi has taken her journey and lessons learned and carefully crafted them in written form. With its conversational tone and presentation, it almost feels as if you're sitting down with a friend simply discussing business, making this very approachable. If you're looking for inspiration and insights for success on a small-scale, look no further than Zero to Four Figures.

By the end of the book not only will you have learned a few things along the way, but you'll feel as if you have someone new rooting for you.

Sierra Cotton | Freelance Proofreader & Editor | www.fiverr.com/sieracotton

ZERO TO FOUR
FIGURES

LESSONS LEARNED BY A ~~broke~~ CEO

To my father, my hero.
To my mother, my rock.
To my sister, my everything.

I am, because of you.

TABLE OF CONTENTS

CHAPTER 1: SELF-LOVE

CHAPTER 4: MARKETING

CHAPTER 5: GROWTH MINDSET

CHAPTER 6: MONEY MINDSET

ZERO TO FOUR
FIGURES

broke

LESSONS LEARNED BY A CEO
^

PRITHVI MADHUKAR

INTRODUCTION

"If I were to... just stop walking in the middle of the road, when the light turns green...

...Would the pain finally stop?"

Well, that would have made a very short book had I chosen a different path that day. I joke about it right now, but I can honestly say it was one of the lowest points in my life and one of the most brutal phases I've ever gone through.

However, out of that phase came the most amazing decision of my life—to start my entrepreneurial journey.

As I look back almost three years later, there is nothing I would have wanted to do differently.

If I had to go through it all over again, I would. It sounds crazy, but it's true because that phase led to me finding myself and my life's purpose.

As I write this book, I'm a four-figure business owner.

Yes, four.

You're thinking of closing the book right now, aren't you? I mean, why wouldn't you?

There are thousands of books written by seven and even eight-figure business owners. Why would you want to read a book by a four-figure business owner?

Should I have waited until I became a six-figure business owner and then written a book?

No, I don't think so.

When I started this journey in September 2019, there were months I couldn't earn a single dollar, let alone make three figures a month.

I'm not a business owner who went viral within the first couple of months and suddenly hopped from three figures a month to seven. *(There's nothing wrong with that, but it's a different strategy when you skip the steps of gradual growth.)*

I'm painfully aware of how I earned each dollar leading up to consistent four figures and how much work it took for me to convince every follower/subscriber/listener to follow my social media pages. I know every bit of backend systems I had to set up from scratch to steadily grow my business. I know exactly how much effort went into every sale and how I *slowly* increased my monthly income from zero to one to two to three and now to four figures.

I'm proud of where I am today on this entrepreneurial journey and how far I've come. I'm going to shout at the top of my roof, "I'm a Four-Figure Business Owner Today!"

Let me tell you why I think I'm successful. As of August 2022, for three years, I've been sitting with my laptop in one of the BRICS countries[1], setting up an entire company in a first-world country, bringing my business to a point where I'm consistently earning four figures in one of the world's strongest currencies. In my opinion, that is a pretty big success. So no, I don't need to wait till I hit six or seven-figure months to feel successful. I have my own milestones, and I'll choose to celebrate the wins I have defined for myself.

I've also learned that it is an entirely different ball game navigating through the first few figures. There are few visible validations of each decision you make during this phase, and most of the time, it can feel like everything is at a standstill. It's easier to give up during this stage because, for the most part, the return on investment, be it for your time, money, blood, sweat, or even tears, doesn't show up significantly in this phase. The return on investment of everything you give to the beginning stages comes back to you in multiple folds during the following stages of your business. While that instills hope, it also means you must keep going even though it may look like there's no light at the end of the tunnel. Trust me, that requires some serious mindset, marketing, and business strategy shifts.

What I've noticed is that most entrepreneurs quit during this stage. It's not

---

[1] Term coined by Global Economist Jim O'Neill in his paper: Sachs, Goldman. "The world needs better economic BRICs." *Goldman Sachs, Global Economics Paper* 66 (2001).

their fault; the beginning stages of this journey are just that damn hard.

In the last three years of helping sixty-plus entrepreneurs and solopreneurs as my clients, I have watched literally 90% of them quit, 5% disappear from the face of the earth, and only the remaining 5% determined to pull through.

I'm not saying that the people who quit were wrong; I'm saying that I understand where they were coming from. I know the urge to wake up one morning and quit this journey in frustration. I understand their decision to go back to a steady, secure 9-to-5 job instead of dealing with the turmoil that comes with the entrepreneurial territory. I'm saying I understand the sense of dread one experiences when they keep putting in the effort only to feel like they haven't moved an inch from where they started. I also know how difficult it is to stick by this journey when everyone around you is talking about how awesome it is to hit six to eight figures while no one even bothers to look at you when you're at any stage before those six figures.

It pains me that no one even talks about this phase, especially when *they are in this phase*. Entrepreneurs are so embarrassed by their perceived lack of success that they don't want to discuss where they are. Most feel confident talking about their entrepreneurial journey only when they've hit six or seven figures.

I don't think that's a healthy mindset to be in. As much as I am in awe of people who are at six to eight figures, I don't think we as entrepreneurs should be talking in hushed tones about where we're currently at.

Because entrepreneurs rarely talk about the initial phases while they are in it, it creates a very distorted view for everyone else out there. I also think that once you surpass the initial few figures and get into the higher ones, things can get a little blurry about how you grew in the beginning stages. Also, the mindset, strategies, and thought processes in the beginning stages of growing your business are very different from the following stages.

Growing from zero to seven figures is a long journey, and without acknowledging your wins along the way, it is harder to keep up with self-motivation.

It is easy to feel you haven't done anything significant, even though you managed to grow a business from zero to maybe three, four, or even five figures.

That's not right. That's not right at all.

These *are* success stories.

We should encourage more entrepreneurs to be proud of wherever they are, whether zero figures or seven figures. We need more entrepreneurs to normalize earning *Zero to Four Figures* because that *is* part of their fantastic journey.

Yes, you will get to seven or eight or even nine figures someday, but today, *today*, you are here, and that's worth every celebration, every bit of pride, and every sense of accomplishment as well.

It is time to change the narrative of your entrepreneurial journey and see yourself as the success you already are, regardless of which stage of the entrepreneurial journey you are at.

When I started out, what frustrated me was the lack of books that focused on the very beginning stages of entrepreneurship. I would read these amazing books by seven or eight figure business owners and feel so inspired, but when it came back to me *actually* sitting at my desk, working on growing my business, I would have these imaginary conversations with the authors of the books:

"Alright, it's awesome that you got to eight figures. I'm hopeful I will get there, but... How did you get to three figures?

How about earning four figures consistently?

Why isn't anyone talking about this? Why isn't anyone hyping up four figures?

Are seven figures the milestone I need to wait to celebrate? Or even say that

I am successful?"

Frankly, no one knows how to navigate the first few figures because there isn't much written about those initial stages. That's precisely why I decided to write this book.

Through this book, I'm hoping to convey the message that even though you may feel that you can't celebrate your success because of what society dictates, you will stop caring about it and celebrate your journey anyway!

I hope that by writing this book, the average number of entrepreneurs quitting during the beginning phase of the entrepreneurial journey will lower.

I mean, I'm *literally* writing an entire book just to hype my consistent four-figure months!

I also wanted to write this book, so I wouldn't forget the lessons I learned in the first few stages. As I grow as a business owner, I'm sure my strategies, thought processes, and mindset will evolve. As a four-figure entrepreneur and business owner today, this book shows how far I've come and the changes I've made to get here.

Now is this book going to help you? I have no idea.

What I do know is that this book is my story.

This book is a compilation of the lessons I've learned during my entrepreneurial journey so far. This book covers how I navigated the beginning stages and the challenges I've faced. I talk about my mistakes and the strategies that led to some of my breakthroughs.

Not only have I shared the stories that led to the lessons learned, but I have also shared my original models, performance tools, and learning tactics for you to implement on your entrepreneurial journey. While every entrepreneurial journey is unique, I know what I share in this book will be a good starting point for your journey.

If anything, I know this book will comfort all digital entrepreneurs and let them know they aren't alone in their journey. This book will show you that somewhere out there in the world, there's a digital entrepreneur, albeit a little quirky, who knows what you're going through and is rooting for you!

If by reading this book, you are convinced to have faith in the process and pull through the roughest times of your entrepreneurial journey, then I believe my work here is done.

This book is divided into chapters which are the main areas that I believe to be integral for the holistic growth of any entrepreneur.

These chapters are further divided into sections. Each section has a story leading to the lesson I learned.

While you can hop over to whichever section you'd like, I recommend reading the book once from start to finish, as there is a flow to it. After that, you can re-read the sections that resonate with what you are currently dealing with.

If you'd like to implement my original models, performance tools, or learning tactics, I have supporting workbooks and resources to help you.

You can check out this link to gain free access to your book bonuses: *www.themarketingnomad.co/zero-to-four-figures*

Before we get to the lessons, let me share the circumstances that led to the start of my entrepreneurial journey.

It's got drama; it's got intrigue, but best of all, it's got a twenty-something-year-old Indian girl who had no idea how her life would change—for the better.

In my opinion, every entrepreneurial journey has that one moment, that one moment when the future entrepreneur gets really fed up with contemplating, puts their foot down, and says, "You know what, I don't care! I'm doing this!"

I'm proud to say that happened to me too.

But before we get to me yelling *"I DON'T CARE!"*—a phrase that exasperated my mom during my teen years—let me rewind a bit.

zup zup zup

That's the rewind button. At least that's what it sounds like in my head.

Let's just… uh, roll with it, okay?

SEPTEMBER 2018

I had just completed my Master of Business Administration with a concentration in Marketing from Rochester Institute of Technology (New York, USA) a few months earlier. I was given one year of Optional Practical Training (OPT)[2] as part of the international student visa perks in the United States of America.

Let me find an analogy to explain what the OPT feels like to every international student eligible for it.

You know those optional free breakfasts you get when you stay at a hotel? You can choose to take up their offer, or you can choose not to. But 99.99% of the time, you take their offer up. In fact, you even build your entire itinerary based on the free breakfast timings—so you feel like you're getting the best bang for your buck. It also helps you feel better about the hole burning in your pocket after the hotel stay.

OPT is exactly like that. If you meet the eligibility criteria, the OPT allows a student on a valid F1 (student) visa to work in the United States for a year.

You can choose to use it or not. If you'd like to opt for it, you must apply just before graduating. Upon your graduation, the OPT is granted to you on

---

[2] *Optional Practical Training (OPT) for F-1 Students.* (2022, May 18). USCIS. https://www.uscis.gov/working-in-the-united-states/students-and-exchange-visitors/optional-practical-training-opt-for-f-1-students

the condition that you find a job within 90 days in your field of study. You must leave the country if you fail to secure a full-time job within those 90 days. Should you choose not to apply for the OPT, you must leave the country within 60 days of graduation.

If you graduated from a non-STEM program like my MBA program, there is no extension for the OPT. Once you've used up the one year given to you by the OPT, either your employer will extend your stay by sponsoring another visa, or again, you must leave the country. If you graduated from a STEM (Science, Technology, Engineering, Math) program, you are given a STEM OPT extension after your one-year OPT is up. The STEM OPT extension is a twenty-four-month training time under the F1 visa.

If you're an international student eligible for the OPT, you're most likely going to make the most out of OPT just so you have a chance at the American dream. Working under OPT helps you feel less guilty about how much the last two years of your master's degree cost.

Add in looming high currency conversion rates, and voila! You've got an international student in desperate need to earn in USD so they can get back part of the money they spent for their education.

I saw my friends from STEM programs get jobs in a New York minute, so of course my ridiculous optimism had to pop in and make me believe my life would pan out the same way.

It did not.

I'd always reach the last round of interviews with a bright smile, feeling quite pleased as I saw my interviewers' faces. They were clearly impressed by my marketing knowledge and business acumen. Just as I would begin to feel that this interview was a sure shot, I'd snap back to reality upon hearing my *most* dreaded question:

"But... you would need sponsorship for continued employment?"

The next few moments would play out the same in every single interview.

"Yes, I would. I have one year of OPT, but after that, I'll need to be sponsored for the H-1B visa."

"Only one year?"

"Yes."

"And you don't get the two-year extension visa?"

"No, I don't."

Awkward silence.

Smiles would falter.

There would be looks exchanged between the interviewer and the intern taking notes of the meeting.

Furious typing would fill the room from the intern to my right on her laptop.

There would be no further questions, and the meeting would end abruptly.

After some polite thank yous and well wishes, I would walk out their door.

Barely an hour later, almost like clockwork, I'd hear a Gmail notification on my phone, just as I would be pushing the door to my home:

"We regret informing you..."

It was challenging for me to find a job after my MBA program because companies were not so open to sponsoring a work visa for me after just one year of working for them vs. three years with my STEM friends.

Not just that, the H-1B work visa process was a lottery, which meant there was still a chance that I would not be able to work for them after a year. Considering the resources a single hiring process needs, they were hesitant to consider an international student from a non-STEM program.

I didn't need an MBA degree to tell me that the odds were not in my favor. Still, I didn't lose hope and continued applying for jobs.

As my ninety-day deadline approached, I mentally prepared myself to look for jobs in India and other countries. By "mentally prepare" I mean crying into my pillow or furiously applying to jobs. There was *nothing* in between.

With twenty days left before my student visa expired without the OPT in effect, I flew from Rochester to Long Island, New York, for a face-to-face interview with a top solar firm in the state.

As usual, I had done my research on the company before the interview. I identified their strengths and potential opportunities, reviewed their current marketing campaigns, etc. I even made a list of my own suggestions for the company in a three-page word document with corresponding figures and charts. True MBA style!

I walked into their office with my signature bright blue file that had my handwritten notes and printed suggestions for the company. I met with the CEO and the Marketing Manager. After an hour of interview, I could sense they were very impressed with me, and much, much later, my Marketing Manager (one of the interviewers) would tell me she knew right off the bat I was going to be a CEO someday. I guess she saw something in me I hadn't realized at the time.

Since the visa situation was my Achilles' heel, I felt insecure. I thought it was best to bring my visa situation to their attention so I would not get my hopes up too high. To my surprise, they still seemed enthusiastic about having me on their team, and they were open to the idea of sponsoring my work visa a year down the line. I thanked them for their time and walked out of their office confidently.

The company doors opened to a parking space right outside. I had barely taken two steps into the parking space when it hit me—a weird, tingling feeling, that feeling where I knew things were finally looking up for me.

You might assume the tingling feeling would stay nice and fuzzy, making you feel safe and happy, right?

Nope, that did not happen.

The tiny tingling feeling started snowballing into full-blown panic.

Technically this was my last shot. Each set of interview rounds with a company took about a month from start to finish, and with the clock ticking on my student visa, I knew I wouldn't be able to attend an interview with another company in the US.

I had to go back to Rochester and start packing. Either to move to Long Island or back to India.

I knew my life would dramatically change after this, and I was overwhelmed by the amount of uncertainty ahead of me. I needed to catch my breath.

There was a grocery store right beside the company. I thought it would look weird if I started bawling in the middle of a parking lot, so I took a shopping cart lying outside. I walked into the store, pretending to be someone with watery eyes who was also casually shopping for avocados. I seemed to fit into the persona I had in my mind, and I felt confident I had fooled everyone at the store.

Once I caught my breath and had a few avocados in my shopping cart as proof I was indeed shopping and not crying, I called my parents and told them I thought the interview went well. Like every conversation with my typical Indian parents about my previous job interviews, we spoke at length. We dissected every question I was asked and every answer I gave. I even specified how I thought my tone was and how I felt about the entire experience. Just by talking to them, I calmed down. Since I was feeling better, I suddenly became more aware of myself standing awkwardly in the cereal aisle.

Not wanting to be mistaken as someone lurking in a grocery store, I walked straight to the cashier's counter and bought the avocados I had mindlessly picked. With my three avocados and a blue file in my hand, I took an Uber to the John F. Kennedy Airport and headed back to Rochester.

Don't worry; things take a happy turn now.

After one more informal interview with other team members at the company, I received my offer letter with September 24, 2018, as my start date. My international student visa was to expire on October 1, 2018. Talk about cutting it close.

I quickly packed my stuff from Rochester into about twenty U-Haul boxes, rented a bright blue Ford EcoSport from Enterprise, a car rental company, and was on my merry way to Long Island.

I rented a studio apartment for myself, bought a Honda Civic to travel to work, and was very happy in my own bubble. I was living the life.

The next few months went by smoothly. Nothing out of the ordinary. Just a girl in her mid-twenties enjoying New York City and the beautiful sandy beaches on Long Island, making new friends, and working at a company she loved.

Exactly eight months later, my life flipped upside down.

THE CRASH

I know it's only been a few pages, but do you remember when I talked about the H-1B visa and how I only had one chance to get it because my master's degree was a non-STEM program?

I'm going to assume you are nodding your head yes.

It's good you remember because with all the fun I was having on Long Island, I had almost forgotten it was time for me to apply for the H-1B visa.

So, in April 2019, my employer applied for my H-1B visa.

In 2019, the USCIS received 201,011 H-1B petitions. From that, a total of 85,000 were projected to be processed.[3]

I thought my H-1B visa would get processed. Even in my worst nightmares, I couldn't fathom leaving the country and job I loved.

I didn't have a Plan B at this point. I didn't even have a Plan A. I didn't even think I needed a plan.

My luck couldn't be that bad, I thought.

---

[3] *USCIS Completes the H-1B Cap Random Selection Process for FY 2020 and Reaches the Advanced Degree Exemption Cap.* (2019, April 11). USCIS. https://www.uscis.gov/archive/uscis-completes-the-h-1b-cap-random-selection-process-for-fy-2020-and-reaches-the-advanced-degree

But that's the thing about luck, I guess. It drops you like a hot potato when you start to get overconfident about it.

Heads up, here's the part of the story when my life flips upside down.

The USCIS sends the receipt notices to notify people that their H-1B application is being processed. By end of April 2019, 90% of my friends had received their receipt notices. The remaining 10% weren't too concerned because they had the option of STEM extension and had two more attempts.

Now, once all the processing receipt notices are sent, the USCIS then starts returning the applications that weren't processed. By the time you get the confirmation that your application wasn't processed, it's a few months down the line and right about the time when your OPT expires.

Until then, you're in limbo because you keep hearing this one random person screaming on the online forums that they got their receipt notice in July, which is supposedly beyond the standard time frame. This makes you believe that maybe your receipt notice was just delayed.

It's the hope that really gets you.

It was because of this very hope that I started getting panic attacks. The magnitude of these was insane. My heart would suddenly start beating fast, seemingly with no trigger, and I would just freeze.

Mind blank.

Or sometimes, I would start thinking about what would happen if I had to leave all my friends and my job, and I would begin to sob out of nowhere— Driving back from work, in the shower, while cooking, or even when I was sitting at the laundromat, waiting for my clothes in the dryer. I would become overwhelmed in the middle of the grocery store and would have to grab the handle of my shopping cart to keep me from falling to the ground from the sheer exhaustion of being in constant panic and anxiety.

By mid-May, I had decided enough was enough.

I couldn't keep living in hope, being anxious twenty-four/seven, and having panic attacks almost every single day.

I just woke up one day and thought I should snap out of hope. No hope meant no panic attacks. I thought that meant I would go back to leading my normal life.

But I didn't *snap* out of hope. What I thought was snapping out of hope was me jumping right into a dark place. This brought a new set of problems I was completely unprepared for.

I would go through the motions of the day like a robot. I could only feel pain. Now that I had given up hope, it was clear that my future was no longer what I thought it would be. I knew what was inevitable, and my body would be in physical pain each time I thought about what would happen. I started shutting people out and kept to myself.

I wondered why this was happening to me. What had I done to deserve this?

I had finally gotten my life together, found a career path I loved, and was secure about the direction I wanted to take my life. I was so passionate about marketing and was very happy.

I just couldn't understand it.

Was I not meant to be happy at all? Was my entire life meant to be one painful episode after the other? Why were there so many painful lessons?

None of my friends were going through this. When was I going to get my respite from pain? My heart and my soul were *so* tired. So tired of fighting constant battles, trying to find the light, and just... being in pain. I could see people around looking at me with pity, with the same thought running through their minds,

"She's done for."

I don't know why, but I felt so humiliated. I thought I was letting my parents down after they had spent their hard-earned money on my tuition fees for my MBA program.

Here's partially why this affected me so much: In the society I grew up in, there's a common misconception that you must be in a particular country, in a particular field, and in a particular company to reach the top or be "successful". For the longest time, I thought the same too. I thought I wouldn't be successful anywhere else because all my life, the only thing I heard people say was, "If you're not in this or that country, then you can't be successful".

This toxic thought pattern fueled my pain.

Dark thoughts started enveloping my mind. Instead of finding ways to work through the pain and move past it, I started looking for ways to end the pain once and for all. What was the point of working through pain if all it did, was come back? I declared to myself in frustration.

I began to feel that nothing ever went my way, and I became very angry with my fate. As the weeks passed, my resentment only grew stronger.

Sometime in mid-May 2019, I was trying to cross the road to get to Chipotle, my literal favorite place in the world, when this random thought occurred:

"If I were to... just stop walking in the middle of the road, when the light turns green...

...Would the pain finally stop?"

What scared me wasn't the thought of ending my pain permanently. By this time, these thoughts filled my head at every possible low moment.

But it was different this time. This particular moment was different. This time, I was one second away from actually doing it. My thoughts were extremely close to becoming actions, and I freaked out. Even as I write this book a good three years later, I still shudder at the thought of how close I was to making the worst decision of my life.

I crossed the road and stood in front of Chipotle, staring at my reflection on the glass door in shock. My hands were shaking.

This wasn't right. The fact that I was close to acting on my thoughts was a wake-up call for me. But what could I do? I didn't know how to deal with this. I was lost. I couldn't see a way out of feeling hopeless about my future.

I didn't go into Chipotle that day. I felt nausea from sheer fear about what had just happened. I went straight home.

Lucky for me, my younger sister, Pinky, was in town for three months, helping me pack and move out of Long Island. She had been around for two weeks, but I hadn't thought to tell her about what I was going through.

As the elder child, I had an aversion to depending on her. Until then, I thought the responsibility of being an elder sibling meant that my younger sibling could rely on me for support, but not the other way around. I decided to remove this mind block as I was desperate. Pinky was the only person I felt comfortable sharing my thoughts with, and I was worried about what would happen if I delayed talking about this.

My need for support outweighed my need to maintain my image as an elder sister, so that night, while we were lying in bed, I gathered the courage to tell her what I was going through. I mentioned every single thought that was running through my mind. Even the ones I was very ashamed of.

Once I got over the initial hesitation of getting my thoughts out, I couldn't stop. I hid nothing. Pinky just listened. I'm not sure how much of it she got between my sobs. I'm surprised I was even able to say anything in that state.

There was one part of the conversation that stood out to me:

"Pinky... I don't know what to do. I don't know what to do now. I don't know what to do next. I can't even see a path in front of me. I just... I just don't know how to get past this."

Silence.

And then she wobbled a bit, turning her whole body to face me. She hugged me tight, and I could hear her say,

"You know that's okay, right?"

"What... What do you mean?"

"I mean... This is some pretty big stuff; if you don't know what to do, that's okay. You don't have to figure it out today or tomorrow, or even by the next month. So... you know, take your time."

It wasn't just her words but *how* she said them that hit me hard. She said it in such a simple and calm way that made me feel as though it was normal to feel lost, that it was okay for me to feel confused for a while and that I didn't have to feel guilty about not knowing what to do.

Hands down, sharing these dark thoughts with someone who loved me has been the most courageous thing I've ever done in my life. That night marked the turning point of my life and is the very reason this book—or even I, for that matter—exist.

The thoughts that were once swirling in my head were starting to disappear.

Now I'm no licensed therapist nor a trained psychologist, and each person's path is different, but what I truly advocate for is finding the courage to ask for help.

Now that my mind was cleared, I began to accept being in limbo until I figured out my next step. I relaxed a little knowing my mind would find signs to show what my next steps should be.

Here's the best part: I didn't just get one sign. I got three.

THE RISE

My conversation with Pinky happened on a Sunday night, and I woke up feeling a bit vulnerable the next day. Every single thought was no longer in my mind but out in the open and in front of me to analyze. As the week passed, I started to feel like my old self again. Now that I knew I didn't need to have everything figured out, it had taken the massive pressure off me.

Even though it may have been coming from a good place, people's pity no longer bothered me. Just because I didn't figure it out at the moment didn't mean I would never.

Maybe it was my confidence coming back, but there was this tiny, new positive thought in my mind:

"You know what, I don't care where I am in the world; I AM going to make it big!"

By the end of that week, I had serendipitously bumped into not one but three entrepreneurs looking for full-time jobs. Now *I* was intrigued.

I knew from a very young age I would start my own company someday. After seeing three entrepreneurs in the same week, I knew it couldn't be a coincidence.

I felt that maybe I was being nudged to see what my next steps could look like. My mind started to play around with the idea of starting my own company immediately rather than five to ten years down the line.

I had the privilege of spending time with each of the entrepreneurs I met that week. I asked them how they'd started their journey, what happened along the way, and how they felt about their entrepreneurial journey. I even asked them if it was easy enough for me to do it. Each one of them told me that it was easy, and I could *totally* do it if I wanted to.

That was, of course, absolute BS—why else would they be looking to quit their entrepreneurial journey and apply for a full-time job instead?

I realized later that the biggest well-kept secret of the entrepreneurship journey is—and I have to tell you this because this is a tell-all book after all—that part of the initiation process of becoming an entrepreneur involves learning how to say, "We're *doing grrrrreat*," especially when everything around us is in flames.

Bonus points if we complement our words with convincing hand gestures.

That's what those three entrepreneurs did as well. It wasn't working well for them, and they were looking for a more stable income. But they couldn't bring themselves to tell me, so instead, they told me it was easy and that I could do it.

Back to the story:

So, at this point, you have to understand I was really, really—and let's add one more—*really* desperate to pick on any sliver of hope to turn my life around. Yes, the most practical way to look at this would have been to see the three entrepreneurs as people looking to move out of their respective ventures and trying to get full-time jobs.

Did I see it that way? Nooo, of course not.

The dreamer and optimist in me took this situation to mean that these three entrepreneurs had dared to take a chance on what they loved and had come out of it with no regrets. I also saw it as a decision that was not permanent nor irreversible. If I pursued something on my own and it didn't work out, it wasn't like I couldn't just get back out there and look for a full-time job instead.

In other words, there was no lasting damage and no regret. So, if I were to give points out, it would be:

Entrepreneurship	10
Me Moping	-10
Normal Route	0

It was right at this moment I got to use the famous winning line for every entrepreneur, and I said,

"I DON'T CARE; I'M GOING TO DO THIS!"

I'm telling you, as I write this book, it has become increasingly clear to me that if I had not made every single decision I have since this turning point, you'd easily be staring at blank pages right now. And probably demanding your money back too.

I mean... you still could, but a girl can hope.

Over the next three months, while I was still in the States, I started to figure out how I would go about this entrepreneurial journey. Before I left New York on September 1, 2019, I had already booked my first job as a marketing freelancer.

This is how I began my entrepreneurial journey. It may have come from a place of pain, anguish, and frustration, but what it eventually led to was so precious and liberating. It took a lot of mindset shifts and various marketing and business strategies to start and grow my business. Now, it's my absolute privilege and honor to share those with you.

Are you ready? Let's go!

CHAPTER 1
SELF-LOVE

I ☑
Me ☑
Myself ☑

The journey starts with you.

1.1

You don't need to have all your ducks in a row.

I went full force ahead with the entrepreneurial journey.

That was one of the best things I did, and I didn't even realize it at the time.

I knew I wanted to start something on my own; I just didn't know what. I was taking a lot of time debating which path I wanted to take.

Did I want to submit resumes on LinkedIn, or was I to heed the signs I was seeing about the entrepreneurship path?

The thinking and rethinking were exhausting.

Around June 2019, I was talking to my bank account manager on Merrick Road, Long Island, about the next steps for my bank account now that I was moving back to India. Here's how the conversation went:

"It's amazing that you're going to be in India! What are you going to do there?"

*Cue pause for two seconds while I decide to change my life's course. *

"You know what? I'm going to start my own Marketing Consultancy Firm."

I don't know if I was fed up with how long I was taking to decide or the sheer exhaustion of organizing and reorganizing my thoughts was getting to me; I just picked one route in that split second.

That was my final decision, and I wasn't going to look back. I didn't know where to start. I just decided on my endpoint, and that was it.

Sounds crazy but let me tell you why that changed the course of my entrepreneurial journey for the better!

I didn't have a plan with solid steps in place, but that meant I was not restricted to the path I thought would bring me success. Without having any preconceived notions of how my journey should go, I made my decisions as and when I needed to, instead of planning too far out.

Not just that, if I had created a plan back then, I'm sure I would have based the plan on the steps taken by other entrepreneurs before me. I would have robbed myself of the opportunity to create a path that was unique to me.

Now, I was open to trying new ideas that had never been done before. There were definitely more mistakes made but seeing how gratifying the last three years of my entrepreneurial journey have been, I wouldn't have it any other way.

Here's the most significant entrepreneurial truth no one talks about—It's impossible and impractical to determine your path beforehand. You really don't know what could lead you to your end goal. You can't draw a map and say, "Alright, I'm going to hit Point A, then Point B, then Point C, then goal!"

Nope, it doesn't work like that. There is no predefined map to follow. It's just a blank sheet of paper with your end goal written. Sometimes even that end goal isn't set in stone and can change throughout your journey. Sometimes it gets scratched out and replaced with something else, putting you on a different path than you set out for.

Having all your ducks in a row before you start your entrepreneurial journey is an illusion. As many preparations or plans or "ducks" as you'd like to have before you start, all of them will vanish when you start walking on this path.

You can watch as many success stories of famous entrepreneurs as possible, but you can't recreate them in the exact same way. Those successful entrepreneurs are where they are today because of the circumstances and resources they had access to. Yes, even the resources they didn't have access to, their innate abilities, skills they picked up along the way, intuition, luck, opportunities they were or were not privy to, and pivots they made at *that* point in time. That's not something you or I or anyone else can recreate. Frankly, their own entrepreneurial journey is not something they can recreate either.

Your entrepreneurial journey is as unique as you because *you* create it as you go.

Once you realize this, not only do you learn that there is no such thing as being fully prepared, but you also stop restricting yourself to only the opportunities you have seen work for others. You start being open to unconventional opportunities that could bring you more success that's never been seen before. It is also important to note that the opportunities that seem ordinary now might have been unconventional when they were created for the first time.

You just have to jump in, but hey, isn't that where all the fun comes from?

1.2

Get the hell out of your way.

The first minute of deciding to be an entrepreneur introduced the feeling of liberation to me.

The next minute, however, came panic.

The minute after that, right on cue, knocked self-doubt.

Did I have the resources to even do this? What would everyone around me say? What if I failed within the first six months? How would I even know if it was a failure? Okay, wait, how would I know if it was a success?

I didn't even know anyone else who had done something like this!

Yes, there were A LOT of famous entrepreneurs in newspapers or magazine articles I would read about, but I didn't personally know any of them! I didn't know what factors contributed to their success or how they started.

I secretly thought they had superpowers, but that's between you and me.

It was also time for me to get real with myself. Did I really have it in me?

And what in the world did "have it in me" even mean?!

As more and more questions plagued me, I felt increasingly hesitant to get going on my next steps.

Instead of spending my time trying to figure out how to get started on my entrepreneurial journey, I started searching for all the means to validate my worth.

I read countless articles on "Character traits of entrepreneurs". Each article had the exact same points, just worded differently. I took those "Do You Have What It Takes to Be an Entrepreneur?" quizzes. These quizzes bore a lot of resemblance to the "Is He Into You" quizzes I took as a teenager, with me trying to manipulate the results to match my hopes. I even read an article about the "Warning Signs You're Not Cut Out to Be an Entrepreneur". There were over thirty traits listed, and I found *one* of them to match my personality.

My heart sank a little. Needless to say, I obsessed over *that* for a few days.

I didn't realize it at the time, but I was procrastinating.

As much as I wanted to step into the entrepreneurial world, I was afraid. My mind had recognized this decision as something that could potentially harm me in the future and was doing everything it could to stop me from moving forward.

I was in my own way.

After a few days of binging articles that did not serve me, I realized I was approaching my decision to become an entrepreneur wrong.

When I started analyzing why I was feeling what I was, I could see that it boiled down to my limiting belief of failing in front of everyone. If I wanted to overcome my fear of stepping into the entrepreneurial world, I had to face my limiting beliefs head-on.

I've always been quite self-aware, and through my early twenties, I had a vague three-step process to help me overcome my limiting beliefs. As much as the process had helped me with my personal life, I wasn't sure if it would work for my professional life. It didn't look like it would hurt to try at the time, so I extended the same three-step process to my business. Of course, I made it a bit more structured.

I noticed a change within a week or two of consistently implementing this framework. I no longer relied on articles to define my worth, and I felt my self-confidence rising. I was ready to take the first step in my entrepreneurial journey.

After recognizing the influence of limiting beliefs and how much they can hinder one's progress in this entrepreneurial journey, I taught my Three-Step Limiting Belief Framework to all my consulting clients. I knew if my clients didn't tackle their limiting beliefs first then no amount of strategies or tactics could bring them the results they wished to achieve.

Since making this mandatory, I've had many clients implement my Limiting Beliefs framework for their business and personal limiting beliefs, and they've been mind-blown by how simple yet effective my framework is.

Given that this framework has changed how I show up for my business, I wish to share it with you too. Here's my Three-Step Framework for Overcoming Limiting Beliefs:

THE "WHAT WHY HOW" FRAMEWORK
FOR LIMITING BELIEFS

For this framework to work, you've got to put in the work. In other words, this is an action-oriented framework. I've given a few examples after the framework description so you can see how to implement it.

Step 1: WHAT Is the Limiting Belief?

I believe this step is crucial because you often may not realize there is an underlying limiting belief. Some limiting beliefs can stem from a previous negative experience. Sometimes, limiting beliefs can arise from the influence of the thought patterns of people around you. In either case, your mind enables a defense mechanism to protect you from potentially harming yourself.

In healthy doses, your mind's self-protection mode keeps you safe and alive. But in some situations, especially when deciding to take a huge risk and leap into the unknown entrepreneurial journey, it can stop you from fully realizing your potential.

Unfortunately, this mode isn't something you get over once and wash your hands off it.

Your mind will consistently put you into this self-protection mode with every new step you take in your journey. Your first task as an entrepreneur is to learn how to recognize the moments you are getting in your own way.

Usually, if you're feeling restricted from doing something that you want to do or is necessary for growth, that's a good sign that you are dealing with a limiting belief. When you understand what your limiting belief is, it becomes easier for you to see how you are blocking your path.

These questions will help you identify your limiting beliefs:

- ◆ Are there any reasons I could be hesitant about growing my business?

♦ Is there something stopping me from taking the action I wish to?

♦ Is there a thought that worries me about my business?

(Note: If you were to implement this for your personal limiting beliefs, you would remove "your business" and add whatever part of your life concerns you. For this book, I'll discuss overcoming limiting beliefs about growing your business.)

Step 2: WHY Do You Feel the Way You Do?

Here's where it starts to get tricky. Identifying the source of your limiting belief helps you emotionally detach from it and logically process it. If a particularly negative experience triggered your limiting belief, then by identifying it, you give yourself a chance to look at the experience in a more positive light. If your limiting belief existed because of the influence of people around you, identifying the source helps you to objectively view their thought patterns and determine the validity of it.

Here are few questions you can ask yourself when you get to this step:

♦ Was there a moment or an incident that triggered this belief?

♦ Am I projecting someone else's limiting belief?

♦ Why do I feel the way I do?

It's crucial at this step to be nice to yourself. I like to call it the "No Judgement Zone". Now the rule of this zone is that when you're in it, no matter what your thoughts are, you have to accept them fully and whole-heartedly. You shouldn't be ashamed of your answer, and you should only have kind thoughts for yourself.

Step 3: HOW Will You Overcome It?

This is the last step, but it usually takes the longest to implement. Once you've emotionally detached from your limiting belief in Step 2, it also becomes easier for you to identify how to overcome it. At this stage, it is vital to figure out actionable steps to take and overcome your limiting belief.

Here are two questions you can ask yourself when you get to this step:

♦ Is there something I can do to stop feeling that way?

Sometimes, depending on the trigger incident, you may not find an actionable step to overcome it. That's completely okay. In those specific situations, ask yourself this question:

♦ If there isn't a way, is there something I can do to keep reminding myself instead?

Now let's take three examples, so you have an idea of how to implement these three steps.

If you visit www.themarketingnomad.co/zero-to-four-figures, you'll get access to a printable workbook to implement this framework.

Example 1:

Let's start with one of the most common entrepreneurial limiting beliefs.

Step 1: WHAT Is the Limiting Belief?

I don't think I can start something on my own.

Step 2: WHY Do You Feel the Way You Do?

I don't have a degree or specialization in my niche, which makes me feel inadequate.

Step 3: HOW Will You Overcome It?

Maybe I can do a certified training course in my niche while setting up my business. *Perhaps I could invest one hour every day to watch free tutorials in my niche and learn as much as possible within a set timeframe.*

By implementing the framework, you have actionable steps to help you overcome your limiting belief.

<u>Example 2:</u>

This method works for any area of your business. Let's take this example of a limiting belief about growing your business's social media account.

Step 1: WHAT Is the Limiting Belief?

I don't think I can grow my business social media account to 1,000 followers.

Step 2: WHY Do You Feel the Way You Do?

I've tried it before, and I only grew by 10 followers.

Step 3: HOW Will You Overcome It?

Maybe I didn't approach it the right way. Let me take some time to research my target audience, identify what kind of content they would like to see, and try again.

<u>Example 3:</u>

This time let's take an example from my own set of initial limiting beliefs. I had started a social media account and was hesitant to post. Once I realized something was holding me back from freely posting, I immediately got to work and started writing my thoughts for each step.

Step 1: WHAT Is the Limiting Belief?

I think people get annoyed when I post stuff about my business.

Step 2: WHY Do You Feel the Way You Do?

There was one business account I followed, and they posted way too much. I did get irritated and unfollowed them. I don't want my followers to feel that way about my business.

Step 3: HOW Will You Overcome It?

I could do some research about industry standards. I could also talk to my followers and gauge their expectations for my social media account. Not just that, I also need to set expectations for my followers, so they aren't frustrated by my posting schedule.

Being an entrepreneur is, first and foremost, getting to know who you are as a person. You have to take the time to understand yourself—What are your strengths, your weaknesses, your limiting beliefs, how your thought process works, what works for you, and what doesn't. If you don't know who you are, you may not know *how* to utilize your strengths to the fullest potential. Without recognizing your limiting beliefs, you'll continue to work in a pattern that hinders your business growth.

A successful entrepreneur is not someone without any weaknesses or any faults or someone who does not make any mistakes. A successful entrepreneur is someone who knows themselves so well that they know how to get out of their own way to propel their business forward.

So, which parts of yourself will you be getting to know today?

1.3

You need to be 100% sure you'll see your vision through.

As an MBA graduate, I was painfully aware of everything that could go wrong in the business world.

Not all entrepreneurial stories are success stories, and I knew I was taking a chance.

As I was setting up my freelance profiles in July 2019, it dawned on me that even though I knew I was taking a more complicated route, I had no clue *why* I chose it. So, I sat at my study table with a blank book and pen in my hand, trying to understand my vision for this journey.

What did I want out of this journey? Why was I even considering it? Really, I could just submit a few resumes and get a full-time job again, so what difference was this journey going to make to my life?

Like in all my engineering laboratory oral examinations, I drew a blank.

I sat there for an hour. I doodled at the corner of the page. It came out quite impressive. I appreciated my self-proclaimed artistic abilities for a while.

Then I decided to write down the questions in my head to answer them. This was a habit I had picked up during my engineering days when I couldn't keep up with the rest of the class and I had a bunch of questions swimming in my head.

So, I wrote:

What's your vision for your life?

I pondered for a bit and wrote an answer to that.

Well, I want to travel the world. I've always wanted to do that. Not just two-week vacations that come with a full-time job, but more. I want to travel a few places a year and stay at each place for an extended period.

That was an excellent answer to the question, I thought. I felt satisfied with my response, so I asked myself the following question:

Is that the only vision?

No, that's not my only vision. I spent many years feeling lost during my engineering days and finding my passion for marketing made me feel like I could breathe again. I don't want to let that go. It's such a beautiful gift to be passionate about something, and I want to continue in marketing.

Then why entrepreneurship?

I want to help businesses across the world. I don't want to restrict the use of my knowledge to just one industry. I really think I was meant to make a difference on a larger scale.

Those three answers helped me create the vision for my entrepreneurial journey. I knew that regardless of what step I would take next, it would always be something in the direction of enabling me to have the freedom to travel while helping businesses across the world.

Now I couldn't promise myself I would be successful on this journey. What I could promise myself was that regardless of whether this journey led to a success or a failure, I would see my vision through.

I had no idea what I would do next or how I would realize my vision, but I knew I would give it my best shot.

That simple promise gave me a different approach while I navigated the difficult times on the journey later on. I'd remember this promise, calm myself down, and brainstorm ways to overcome the problem or work around it. Being in this mindset made me more determined to try every possible way out instead of giving up at the first sign of trouble. Not just that, this commitment to my vision made me very conscious of every step I took from that moment on. Each time I would think of a new direction for my journey, this question would pop into my head:

"Am I in alignment with my vision?"

When starting out on this entrepreneurial journey, it helps to ask yourself *why* you're doing what you are doing.

A few questions you can ask yourself are:

- What's the vision I have for my life?

- How will this journey get me there?

- What will this journey bring that a 9-to-5 job won't?

- *How* committed am I to see this vision through? *Why* am I committed to see this vision through?

Trust me, very often on this journey, you're going to find yourself asking yourself, *"Why am I doing what I'm doing?"* Having an answer helps you stay on course.

And we all want to stay on this journey for as long as we can, don't we?

If you visit www.themarketingnomad.co/zero-to-four-figures, you'll get access to a printable workbook to help you find your vision.

1.4

Who is the person you need to be?

When I decided to take on this journey, I knew I had it in me to get to where I wanted to be.

It's safe to say that I had considerable confidence in myself. Unfortunately, I missed out on something important.

While I knew I had all the skills, knowledge, determination, discipline, and passion for being a successful entrepreneur, I had to become someone who could use my strengths to help me succeed.

In August 2019, I was still reeling from the pain of my dreams crashing. I was trying to cope that I would have to start a new life in another country, far away from my best friends, in a few short weeks.

I kept envisioning every friend of mine moving on to more successful jobs and having their dream life while I was nowhere to be seen. It was difficult for me to look at my life positively.

Sometimes I just didn't want to get out of bed because I didn't want to face reality. I'd skip breakfast and eat pizza for lunch and ice cream for dinner every day for the two weeks leading to the day of my flight back to India. I often stared blankly at the wall, soaking myself in all the self-pity I could muster.

I was crying a lot. I'd walk by the park near my studio apartment, realize it was one of the last few times I'd ever get to see it, then break down. I would normally be breathing one minute only to feel my heartbeat suddenly rise. Instinctively, I would clutch my chest because I was having a full-blown panic attack. I'd sleep most of the day, waking up only to do essential tasks like packing my stuff or talking to buyers about the things I couldn't take with me to India. I lost interest in living life. I just didn't want to bother anymore.

You might have already guessed—that's not the trait of a person who becomes a successful entrepreneur.

On September 3, 2019, I landed in Bangalore, India, early in the morning. I stayed in my room the whole day and did not come out to talk to my parents or sister.

I knew I couldn't keep myself holed up in my room forever. I don't know if I felt like I wanted to refresh my life because it was a new place or because I was shocked at the shell of a person I had become, but I decided to give myself only twelve more hours of residual crying time.

I even set a rule for myself. After the twelve hours were up, I wasn't allowed to waddle in self-pity. I called it my "feel bad" time. I would be a version of myself that could become a successful entrepreneur.

My first freelancing job was going to start in five days, and I made up my mind to prepare mentally for it.

The same night, I remember getting a pen and a paper.

In the middle of the paper, I wrote, *"Who is the person I need to be?"*

I thought for a few minutes. Nothing came to my mind. I thought maybe I wasn't getting any ideas because the title looked too ordinary, so I drew a cloud around it. That should make my thoughts flow, I thought.

A few more minutes went by. Nothing was striking my mind yet. Then I remembered a very famous entrepreneur, Sara Blakely, Founder of Spanx.

"What are some of the traits I like about her?" I asked myself.

Well, I loved how determined she was. She started from absolutely nothing, and she never gave up. She was disciplined. She believed in herself and her vision. She genuinely wanted to make the lives of women more comfortable and better. In all those years of rejection, she did not wallow in self-pity. She also knew how to live life as a vibrant and fun person.

I saw those qualities in myself, but those qualities were also overshadowed by my pain. Feeling inspired, I began writing. I wrote all my qualities that could contribute to becoming a successful entrepreneur.

Once I started writing, I didn't stop. I started remembering all my strengths and wrote those down. I remembered my weaknesses and wrote suggestions on how to overcome them. If there was a weakness I could not overcome in the immediate time on hand, I wrote down ways to work around it.

In the next two hours, I had a page fully scribbled with information about the kind of person I needed to be to get to where I wanted to be. Having all my thoughts on paper relaxed me a bit. I felt my old self coming back. I put these actionable steps on a post-it and stuck them on a place I could see daily to remind myself.

The following day, I woke up with the sole purpose of just doing the things on my post-its. I didn't focus on anything else. I didn't focus on *why* I was in Bangalore. I didn't focus on *what* had happened. I didn't focus on *how* I would get to where I wanted to be.

I didn't hit everything on those post-its that day, but I did manage to get a few things right.

I got out of bed and made my bed.

I had wholesome meals.

I set up my room and my worktable.

Each day I worked on one new thing on my list. I allowed myself to try a little more with every passing day. Within a few weeks, I had a set routine in the morning. I had created a small marketing plan for my business. I also started creating content and calling myself "The Marketing Nomad".

I just focused on becoming the person I needed to be, and by the time I'd realized what I was doing, I had already made things fall into place. After seeing how effective this practice was, I started to do it every year.

During the few days leading up to each new year, I take a piece of paper. I write the title in the middle of the page, draw a cloud around it, and jot all my thoughts down.

Recently, I added a new question, and that is, *"How?"* After writing about the kind of person I needed to be, I'd ask myself for actionable ways to get there.

For example:

The person I needed to be: More disciplined.

How: Wake up every day at the same time.

I purposely didn't give myself an actual time because I just wanted to start with the smallest step of waking up every day at the same time, regardless of the time. Once I got into the practice of waking at that time, I'd slowly move to wake up at a specific time every day.

The key to this is baby steps. You don't want to get overly excited and skip steps. If you do, then when the excitement wears off, you will go back to the previous version of yourself. We don't want that.

Another example:

The person I needed to be: More knowledgeable.

How: Keep fifteen minutes every day to learn something new.

A funny incident I remember is when I first started the "how" part, I would overdo it. I once put, *"Spend three hours every Sunday to learn something new."*

I didn't even do it for the first Sunday after I wrote that. It was a bigger step than I was ready to take, so I didn't bother.

The key is to find the right balance between an action you're too comfortable with and an action you're not ready for. It takes some trial and error—as you can see with my example—but over time, you will become much more conscious of what you can sustain long term and what you cannot.

The items on your list depend on so many factors, like, for example, what the trait is, the steps you add for yourself, the speed of growth of your business, etc., so of course, the details on your list will change as time passes by. It's good to check your list every few months to see if you're on track.

Another important thing to note is that as you grow, you'll start to be more aware of the person you need to be for your business's next stage of growth, not just the long-term vision you have for yourself. You start to learn more about the strengths and weaknesses you never knew you had, and you build this list upon those newfound traits.

If in doubt, always ask yourself:

- ♦ Who is the person I need to be?

- ♦ How do I get to the person I need to be?

If you visit www.themarketingnomad.co/zero-to-four-figures, you'll get access to a printable workbook to help you understand the person you need to be.

1.5

You get to define your worth and people's access to you.

Everyone has their own insecurities, and I'm not an exception to that.

Let's recap my standing when I started this entrepreneurial journey.

I had an engineering degree from PESIT Bangalore South Campus, a reputed college in India, which meant that I was in a unique position to understand and help engineering-based businesses with their marketing. I had an MBA with a concentration in marketing from the Rochester Institute of Technology, a respectable university in New York, which meant that my marketing strategies were built upon my keen understanding of the foundations of a business. I also had work experience from my time at EmPower Solar, a top solar firm in New York, which gave me a great starting point to hone my marketing skills.

Now to anyone else seeing this write-up, they'd be impressed. Heck, if I were reading this about someone else, I'd be impressed too. That's some good stuff there.

Unfortunately, when I started out, I did not feel this way about myself. I felt massively insecure. In my mind, I was new to the entrepreneurial journey, so that to me meant I didn't know as much as the other seasoned entrepreneurs.

For some reason, I completely forgot my degrees, my knowledge, my experience, my exposure, and my level of expertise. I thought I was only in Year 1 of this entrepreneurial journey, while everyone else was much further along. This thinking pattern transmuted into my actions as an entrepreneur.

Given my insecurity, I felt I needed my clients more than they needed me. I thought they could have hired more seasoned freelancers. Because they chose *me*, I felt I was in their debt. This created a weird need for me to keep going overboard with my deliverables so I would feel assured that they didn't regret choosing me.

Like in every other kind of relationship built on insecurity, it doesn't take too long to become an extremely toxic environment.

Either one of two situations usually play out:

The person on the other side abuses their power, and the one with the insecurity keeps allowing it.

Or the person feeling the insecurity over gives until they break, and the other is left clueless about what happened. I've been in both of these situations since the beginning of my entrepreneurial journey.

In the first situation, one of the clients who had hired me in October 2019 kept giving me more workload throughout our engagement period. The additional work was not mentioned in the scope nor in the contract. This was one of my first jobs as a freelancer, and I was too scared to speak up. I felt that if I asked for compensation, then they might choose to go with another freelancer who could accommodate their additional deliverables without getting compensated for it. I tolerated this for a few weeks. Given the extra workload, I was earning too little per hour. I even thought of quitting the project at one point.

I sought the help of my parents because I knew they had similar experiences before and would know what to do.

Here's something you have to know about my parents. They don't really tell my sister and me what to do. Instead, they give us the best case and the worst-case scenarios for each decision we could make and leave it to us to make our own decisions.

Over the years, it's become easier to tell which decision my parents would like us to make even though they feel they are being "neutral" which is really funny because they don't know that we know what they want us to do. But sometimes, the decisions are such that there isn't really a right way or a wrong way, but just that each decision has its own consequences, and we have to decide if we are ready to face those consequences.

This was one of those cases where there wasn't a right or a wrong decision, but I just had to be prepared for the consequences of whichever decision I chose to make. So, when I told my parents what was happening, they listened, and we talked about my possible options.

One option was to speak up and let my client know I was happy to take on more workload as long as I was compensated. Yes, that meant risking the client ending the contract. That also meant losing out on a potential testimonial. Everyone knows every testimonial's value, regardless of where you are on your entrepreneurial journey.

The second option was to wait till the period of engagement was over, which was December 2019. Then, when it came to renewing my contract, I could give my updated rates and make my terms clear if more work was to be added to the scope while the project was in progress.

I had a couple of weeks before the contract ended, so I decided to wait it out. It was hard, and I questioned my decision after two weeks because the additional workload was getting ridiculous. In all fairness, I do not know if that particular client was doing it intentionally or if they were just figuring out new tasks for me as the days went by.

When you're in a situation like this, it's easy to blame the other person for how they treat us. I actually don't think it is the other person's fault. Even while writing this, I don't blame my client at all. It was on me to define my worth. It was on me to set my boundaries. It was on me to speak up. I had to let them know what I would and wouldn't allow. It was on me to define their access to me. It was on me to let my client know how I wanted to be treated.

It was on me, period.

This was a heavy lesson, not just for my business relationships but also for my personal relationships.

Once the contract was over, my client asked me to send a revised agreement. I did. I added the new terms and conditions. I updated my rates to match my educational degree and experience. The client did not move forward with me due to budgetary restrictions, but I was at peace with their decision because I knew I was aligned with my worth.

The second situation played out around January 2020, and it was slightly different. This time, it wasn't my client asking for more, but I over-giving to a point where I exhausted myself unnecessarily.

Around this time, I had clients on the other side of the world. This meant there was a time difference between us. When I started, I did not want to lay any time restrictions on my clients. I didn't want them to feel inconvenienced that they were hiring someone who wasn't in their country. If I look back now, I know I was heavily insecure about the fact that there were freelancers in their respective countries who were available. I didn't want my clients to second guess their decision to hire me.

I would wake up at 3 a.m. to have calls with my clients. I would go to sleep at 6 p.m. and wake up at 12 a.m. just to have a call with my clients. If they wanted two deliverables, I would give ten. If they wanted a small favor from me, I would extend myself without considering my limitations.

It's okay to go above and beyond for your clients, but there is a point where it becomes too much. That's not healthy.

Of course, there's nothing wrong with working on your clients' time zones, and I know there are so many people out there who do. The only difference is that there was an easier way to work things out in my case, and I couldn't see it because I was blinded by my insecurities.

See, even though there was a time difference, there was a time overlap that worked for my client and me. I didn't realize this until my mentor, Chuck, said, *"Prit, YOU get to define what it takes to get access to you. If 8 a.m. to 10 a.m. EST is the time you're comfortable with, set that as your access time. The people who want to work with you will respect that."*

The minute Chuck said this, my mind was blown. I didn't even realize I could set a time of access.

Wait, let me rephrase that—*I didn't think I was worthy of setting a time of access.*

I didn't think there was an option where my client *and* I didn't have to be inconvenienced.

Thus, I started setting my time of access. Initially, I was scared I would lose clients, but nothing happened. My clients were very open to accommodating my time of access and were glad I brought it up.

Eventually, when my business grew and my time was divided between multiple income streams, I became specific about the days I kept for my clients. I was no longer overworking nor inconveniencing myself. I was sleeping well and maintaining a healthy routine. I felt energized to take on more work.

When you enter a relationship feeling insecure, any relationship for that matter, the person who loses the most is *you*. When you know your worth and what you bring to the table, you recognize that the relationship is a two-way street. When you are secure in yourself, you no longer just think about the difference you are making to the other person. You also start to recognize the contribution both of you are making to the relationship. You become aware that you are needed by the other person as much as they are needed by you.

An equal power dynamic is established here, creating a fruitful and long-lasting relationship.

If you'd like to establish better boundaries for yourself, here are a few questions you can ask yourself:

- What will I allow?

- What will I not allow? *(If you're feeling uncomfortable with someone's actions, that's a good sign that it may be something that you will not allow)*

- Am I taking this action because I want to people-please or because I have to do it?

- Am I compromising on my health *(emotional, mental, and physical)* to finish this task?

- If the answer is yes to the above question, how can I change the way I show up so that I'm not compromising?

The simplest way to go about it is to recognize your worth and clearly define what it takes to get access to you. The clearer your boundaries are, the easier it becomes for both sides to work harmoniously.

Better boundaries, better life, right?

1.6

Your business is NOT your identity.

Before starting this entrepreneurial journey, I based my identity on many things that were going well in my life.

I was a Marketing Coordinator at a top solar firm.

I was the girl living her best life in New York.

I was the Indian girl who had found her American Dream.

When my work visa was not processed, everything that I had based my identity on came crashing.

Yes, it was wrong of me to base my identity on my surroundings.

I never took the time to understand who I was without any of the additional layers to my identity.

As I've come to realize now, I did this because I was afraid of what I would see if I looked inward, so I kept adding these layers to make myself feel more secure.

Naturally, I felt a loss of identity when all of it was taken away.

I no longer knew who I was or what I could base my identity on.

Even when everything crashed, I didn't realize I had to look inward and find my identity. I was desperate to cling to something, anything, to base my identity on.

Thus, I latched on to my identity as an entrepreneur. I had chosen not to take the usual employment route but the roller coaster entrepreneurial route. I felt I needed to justify my risk by taking on "entrepreneur" as my identity.

I clung to it for dear life.

Basing my entire identity as an entrepreneur started out with little things. When speaking to people, I would immediately bring up the fact that I was an entrepreneur before they could get a word in. I was so worried that the only thing people would associate my identity with would be someone whose visa didn't get processed, so I would divert their attention to my new role as an entrepreneur.

Then, it got bigger and bigger. Every time something didn't go well in my business, I would feel *I* was a failure. If there was something that I couldn't achieve in my business, I would think it was a testament to me as a person.

As I built my identity around my business, it became more challenging to see who I was without my business. The time I spent on myself and the time I spent on my business started blurring.

Soon, I was either thinking about my business or working on my business. I couldn't relax because my business was always on my mind. I couldn't focus on anything else because if this failed, I would have to feel a loss of identity again, and I was desperate not to let that happen.

I burned out within three months of starting my entrepreneurial journey in January 2020.

I was always on edge because of the constant fear of losing my identity again. I was drained because even when I thought I was taking a break, I was still thinking about my business.

By this time, I had gotten into the practice of journaling. When I looked back at my previous journal entries from the last few months, I saw a disconnect.

My business was my identity, and I couldn't bring myself to separate the two. Each hit my business took felt like a hit to my identity. Immediately, I'd go into a hyper-defensive mode, trying to salvage what I thought was my identity. All my actions towards my business were from a Place of Insecurity, which meant my efforts were not necessarily aligned to the highest good of my business.

It became clear that I had absolutely no idea who I was without my business.

I didn't understand the person I was. I didn't know my strengths or my weaknesses. I didn't know what made *me*, as a person, happy. I didn't know what I liked or what I didn't like. I didn't know what my values were, and I certainly wasn't aware of my beliefs.

All I knew was that I was a business owner, a broke one at that, and I was beginning to realize that *this* couldn't be my identity.

My identity was in me, like a tangled web, and I had to untangle each string.

It reminded me of those times in the Electronics lab during my engineering days when we had to untangle a huge bunch of cords. It would almost seem impossible. First, I'd tug at one cord, follow it to its source, and then move it around the other cords to untangle it. One by one, I'd slowly unravel it and keep it aside.

This was not a very fast process.

Sometimes I'd get frustrated and rapidly shake the bundle of cords in the air. One cord would fly out, hit someone else in the lab, and I would hide under the table so no one would know it was me. I would look at the bundle again, hoping that I had accomplished my goal, but somehow, the bundle would end up more tangled than I started with. Patiently untangling the bundle was usually the easiest way to go about it.

It was the exact same process with finding my identity. I had to find one line of thought, look for its source, and wiggle it a bit to shake off the residue of the influence of my surroundings, be it my job, career, or even the people around me. One by one, I managed to find out each facet of me.

When I started to build my sense of identity, I slowly stopped relying on my business to be my identity. My decisions for my business were based on what I felt was right instead of allowing my insecurities to dictate my next steps. Over one year, I started to feel more secure in myself, regardless of whether things were going okay with my business or not. I had finally separated my identity from my business and created an identity that focused only on me.

Especially when you are an entrepreneur, it's easy to let your business become your identity. It happens even before you know it. Most of the time, we've risked quite a bit to become an entrepreneur. That's why keeping our business as our identity helps us justify the risk we've taken. That's detrimental to our business in the long run, as our decisions are based more on fear than our instincts, rational mind, and/or logic.

Not just that, as time goes on and your identity merges with your business, you will find it hard to separate your business life from your personal life. The line keeps getting blurred until one day, there isn't any line anymore, and you're left wondering why you're feeling so burned out all the time.

In my case, I had to build my sense of identity from scratch. It may or may not be that way for you. Some of you may already have a strong sense of identity. Either way, knowing who you are without your business is essential.

At any given point on this journey, you have to be able to answer this question with ease: if I don't have my business tomorrow, who am I?

1.7

Work to your strengths to achieve success.

One of the biggest mistakes I ever made was thinking that I had to be *exactly* like the successful entrepreneurs I looked up to if I wanted some semblance of success.

The repercussions of this mistake were huge.

When I decided to become a digital entrepreneur, I researched other successful digital entrepreneurs. I watched how they behaved and how they presented themselves to the world. I also observed countless YouTube videos where these entrepreneurs gave tips on being more like them.

The one common thing among the digital entrepreneurs I looked up to was their stoic demeanor. These digital entrepreneurs were formal when they conveyed their messages.

I thought that being formal meant being professional.

I misunderstood that being a digital entrepreneur meant that I had to show the world a formal and stoic version of myself.

My first few YouTube videos were precisely that way. I was formal and stoic. I gave my tips in the format that every other digital entrepreneur gave.

I disliked the version of myself I had presented for those YouTube videos. Even on my Instagram page, I just wasn't myself. I didn't talk about my feelings; I didn't show them my natural personality and just did what everyone else was doing.

Now, I have to mention that I've always been fiercely myself. I've never apologized for being myself or for speaking my mind. I've always been highly confident in my own skin.

But when I started this journey, it wasn't that I wasn't confident about who I was or that I didn't want to be myself. I just thought I had to be a particular kind of person to succeed.

As I was creating content for my YouTube channel, my Instagram page, or my podcast, I always felt so drained. I stopped liking what I was doing, and that was odd.

I loved being in front of the camera. I loved to talk, so it felt unnatural when I wasn't keen on doing it anymore. I brushed these feelings and continued to create content. I did this for a whole year.

100 YouTube videos. Over 200 Instagram posts. Around 30 podcast episodes.

And then I burned out massively in June 2020.

I started hating every single aspect of content creation. I didn't even want to think about creating content anymore. I took a break for two months. When I took that break, I didn't think I would ever get back to it.

After a month, the burnout started to subside. I was beginning to feel like my old self. As I began to analyze why I felt burned out, I looked hard at why I even became a digital entrepreneur.

I started this journey because I wanted to make a difference to the people around me. And yes, I was making a difference with my marketing tips. But that wasn't all I wanted to do.

I wanted to transform the way people thought about their lives.

I wanted them to know they weren't alone in their entrepreneurial struggles.

I wanted to share my ups and downs.

I wanted to be more open about my mistakes and the lessons I had learned.

I felt that that was my calling. I knew I wasn't aligned with my calling by suppressing my true personality. I was unhappy not being myself, and that was one of the factors contributing to burnout.

At the end of the sixty days, I decided to do whatever I wished. It didn't matter to me what anyone thought. I was just going to be myself, and even if I wasn't successful, I'd be content with the fact that I was true to myself.

I started showing up as exactly myself on every platform of mine.

If I messed a word on my podcast episode, I'd laugh it off and continue. Previously, I would rerecord the entire sentence multiple times. Now, I stopped being so rigid about it. The real me didn't care about messing up a word because this way, the episode seemed more natural, and that was also how I would have liked someone else's podcast to be too.

My YouTube videos transformed the most. I started talking about topics that most people didn't talk about. Topics that revolved around leading a more enriched life. I shared my personal life stories as well my business stories. I was completely free and easy by being my quirky self.

I expressed myself through Bollywood dancing on my Instagram page. I started talking more about my feelings and struggles on my Instagram stories. I showed people my sense of humor. I felt so relaxed and happy. I was no longer feeling drained when I was creating content. In fact, I was feeling more energized even though I would be wrapping up a 3-hour content creation shoot. I loved every minute of it.

And just like that, everything changed for me.

People started to understand who I really was. They began to trust me more. They saw how open and transparent I was, and they too, started sharing their own journey with me. The comments I received on my Instagram reels were heartfelt. I started having such beautiful conversations in my direct messages because people resonated with what I spoke. I started meeting more like-minded people, and my inner circle started growing.

I had potential clients reaching out to me, saying they wanted to work with me. My price point was irrelevant to them because they saw the person I was and absolutely trusted that I could bring them the results and transformation they were looking for.

Everything started to feel easy for me. All I had to be, was myself.

This was *my* strength.

My personality was *my* strength.

My sense of humor was *my* strength.

My flair for storytelling was *my* strength.

My passion for Bollywood dancing was *my* strength.

My easy-going nature was *my* strength.

Then why was I going through all that trouble to suppress my strengths?

That's when I understood:

When you're starting out, you're understandably excited. As much as possible, you want to do everything your heroes do. There's nothing wrong with that, except that that can start to cloud your own instincts.

You don't realize that your heroes were working to *their* strengths. They got to their level of success because they based it on their instincts, finely tuned to how *they* were comfortable operating.

That may or may not be what *your* strengths are. That may or may not be something you can keep up long-term. Their strengths could even be the opposite of your nature and comfort level.

When you're not comfortable, it shows. People can easily pick up on that and sense something is off.

As much as you are in awe of your heroes, you must do what works to *your* strengths, not theirs.

If you have a serious demeanor and the hero you admire is chirpy, don't shift your entire personality in your pursuit to emulate them.

If you're a fun-loving, happy-go-lucky person and the hero you admire is rigid, again, don't suppress what makes you, *you*.

When you are yourself, you attract the people who like you for who you are. The kind of people who respect you for the values you have. People who you wish to be around too.

While you can take inspiration from how your hero behaves or what they do, it's essential to be authentic to who you are. There will be some traits that you can try to incorporate but use your discretion.

Ask yourself the following questions:

- ◆ Am I changing who I am by copying this trait of theirs?

- ◆ Does this trait of theirs add value to my life without changing my fundamental core being?

- ◆ Can I keep this up long-term?

- ◆ Do I still feel like myself after adding this trait of theirs to my life?

For example, one of your heroes has a morning routine that improves productivity.

If you're someone who likes routines, then when you choose to incorporate their morning routine into your life, it might make you happier and more content with your life. That's because this trait doesn't fundamentally change your personality and it aligns with your strengths.

However, if you were someone who thrives in fluidity and spontaneity, you would change your core being by trying to incorporate this trait. Eventually, you would feel suffocated, restricted, and resentful. As much as it helps your hero with their own life, it may actually be counter-productive for yours because it doesn't work to your strengths.

There's nothing wrong with trying to be like your heroes, but you've got to pick the traits that work to *your* strengths, not those that suppress them. That's the distinction you need to make when trying to be like your heroes.

After all, shouldn't this journey be about *you*?

1.8

Creating opportunities for yourself is a skill. Hone it.

I've always disliked the phrase *"Opportunity knocks but once."*

It suggests that you've got to be eagerly waiting behind the closed door, literally jumping at any slight noise you hear on the outside.

I don't think that's necessary.

I don't think opportunities knock. I don't believe opportunities exist on their own, floating around in space and waiting for the stars to align to come to you.

I believe we *create* opportunities. I think the power is in our hands to make something out of what others perceive as nothing. That is what truly determines how successful our journey will be.

Do you remember when I mentioned the three entrepreneurs who were getting back into a full-time work life?

Everyone around me saw the interaction as just another interview for the open position. I, however, saw the interaction with them as an opportunity for me to learn about how they started on their own. I even reached out to one of them later for advice on getting started.

I *created* an opportunity there. I created something valuable to me out of a regular interaction. And what do ya know, that interaction planted the seed of entrepreneurship in my mind.

Another example? Alright, here it comes:

In June 2020, I enrolled in a course in which I was one among a thousand students. The course went smoothly.

At that point, I was about a year into my entrepreneurial journey. As with most entrepreneurial journeys, I felt a bit alone as I didn't have anyone around me who understood the ups and downs of the digital entrepreneurship journey. I had a lot of support from my family, mentors, and friends, but as much as they cared for me, it was difficult for them to understand what I was going through.

So, there I was, in a Facebook group with 999 other entrepreneurs. Most of them were digital entrepreneurs like me. Being a part of that Facebook group meant I could create the opportunity to make many friends who were in the same boat as me.

I decided to start chatting with the other students in the course. Whenever I had time, I started answering the questions that were posted to the group, helping other entrepreneurs solve any marketing-related problems.

I didn't stop there. I also shared the lessons I was learning with my business. In no time, I started making friends from across the world. Now, I had friends who understood the unique challenges of building an online business and knew exactly what I was going through.

I no longer felt alone in my journey.

I could have quickly finished the course and been content with the knowledge I had gained. Instead, I *created* an opportunity to meet new people and learn about their entrepreneurial journeys and lessons. I created the opportunity to form healthy friendships and make my journey more enjoyable.

I'm still in touch with most of the people I connected with through the course. We've held accountability sessions. We've held virtual party nights. We've even held virtual meetups to discuss any problems we were facing in our business and to help each other brainstorm ways to overcome those problems. There are even a few of them I've called up in the middle of the day, asking for their advice, not just with my business but with respect to my personal life. They continue to stand by me with the same support and encouragement as I do for them.

Those relationships are priceless to me. The strength of our friendship really amazes me. We come from different countries, ethnicities, races, cultures, social strata, and upbringings, but our passion for making a difference in the world unifies us.

It is these little things that make my journey so beautiful and enriching.

If we must talk about how this helped me in my business, then first off, having a great support system adds to my emotional health, thus allowing me to show up for my business in the best way possible.

Here's another positive thing that's come from the strong friendships that I built through the course:

I launched my own membership program a couple of months after the course and had forty people sign up. Of the forty people who enrolled in my membership program, thirty-five were friends from the course I had enrolled in.

They believed in me, what I had to offer, and the difference I could make in growing their business. That was such an absolute honor for me.

This added so much to my life and business because I believed I could *create opportunities*.

On this journey, it's especially easy to feel dejected. It's incredibly frustrating when you think you must wait for opportunities to come knocking on your door.

You don't have to wait for anything.

You just need to learn how to *create* opportunities for yourself. I know how daunting that can seem, so I've designed a framework to help you with this.

THE 3C FRAMEWORK FOR CREATING OPPORTUNITIES:
CLEAR | CONSIDER | CREATE

The basis for this framework is that, well, you guessed it, *you create opportunities for yourself.* Creating opportunities to better your life is a skill, and applying this framework takes continuous practice to get better at it.

If you visit www.themarketingnomad.co/zero-to-four-figures, you'll get access to a printable workbook to implement this framework.

Now let's get into how to learn the skill of creating opportunities for yourself.

Step 1: Be CLEAR about what you want.

When you're learning to create opportunities for yourself, it is crucial to understand what you truly want.

A few questions to ask yourself at this point:

- ◆   What is the life I envision?

- ◆   How do I see my business going?

- ◆   How do I see myself as a business owner?

- ◆   What additions do I want in my life or business?

The more clarity you can bring to the vision for yourself and your business, the easier it becomes to create the opportunities.

Step 2: CONSIDER the possibilities.

If you're feeling a certain way, it helps to ponder about *why* you are feeling it and what could be a possible solution to ease that feeling. In every situation you find yourself in, take some time to look at the various possibilities of what you can create. See if any of those possibilities match the things you want.

A few questions to ask yourself at this point:

- Is there something more I could make of this?

- How can I make this experience even better for myself?

- Is there a way I could make the most of the resources given to me?

- What additions can I make to my life/business with this?

I'll admit, it takes a while to get the hang of this. What has helped me in the past is looking at people who have had massive success in their life, reading their backstories, and recognizing the instances where they managed to create an opportunity for themselves.

When you start realizing the moments that they created opportunities for themselves, you begin to relate them to your life, making it easier for you to know which opportunity you can create based on the situation you find yourself in.

Step 3: CREATE the opportunity.

Of course, this is the most critical step. You can sit and wonder about all the possible opportunities you can create, but if you aren't getting to work, then it's not going to actualize.

This step usually takes courage. This is also the step that most people abandon because they are afraid the possibilities will not pan out the way they hoped. But here's the thing, it doesn't have to.

Sometimes the opportunity you envision in your head doesn't unfold that way. It's part of the learning process. The important thing is that you took actionable steps to create the opportunity. The more you try to create opportunities for yourself, the more you understand where the gap between your vision and implementation is. As a result, you will keep getting better at reducing the gap as time passes because creating opportunities is a skill.

Through my experience, I've realized that when you create one opportunity, there is always the possibility of creating a few more within the same opportunity itself!

Having an open mind about creating your opportunity can help you be more open to multiple possibilities. Bit by bit, opportunity by opportunity, you realize that it is slowly creating your path to success.

Remember, it is in your power to create the opportunity. You don't have to sit around and wait for one to pass you by. You don't have to look wistfully at your competitors and envy them for their amazing luck or the opportunities that they seem to have.

They created their own opportunities, and so can you for yourself.

Does it not feel amazing knowing that this is in your hands?

1.9

Trust yourself to find a way.

In the last three years, one of the biggest questions I've gotten is, *"How do you do the things that you do?"*

People are often surprised. How did I start my business? Or my YouTube channel? And how did I decide to start my podcast? Set up a digital shop on Etsy? Get brand sponsorships for the social media platforms I'm on? Then earn a modest but consistent income in one of the world's most sought-after currencies?

Here's my answer to that:

I just never felt that anything was stopping me.

Not once did it occur to me that I couldn't do it. I just trusted myself to find a way.

It took me some time to realize that trusting myself was the key to changing my life, so let's rewind.

In August 2019, when it was confirmed that my H-1B visa had not been processed, the rug under me had been pulled, and I was bruised quite badly. I was desperate to gain some semblance of control in my life when I realized, in all my life, there was only one thing that remained constant:

Me.

I realized that the only person consistently showing up through each phase of my life, ready for round 210,498 was me.

Just me.

Even when I was so exhausted from dealing with life, I didn't give up. I was taking deep breaths and picking myself back up slowly.

In all my years, I had never let myself down. Regardless of my external circumstances, luck, fate, or whatever else, the one person I could always count on was myself.

Thus, I began to blindly trust myself.

I began to trust that I would somehow find a way.

I began trusting that my skills, my knowledge, my ability to learn as I go, my resourcefulness, and my intellect were enough for me to achieve what my heart desired and to be able to live the life I dreamed of.

Here's where it starts to get interesting.

I stopped feeling lost about my external circumstances when I started to trust myself. I stopped lamenting my fate for my unprocessed work visa. I stopped envying others for having better "luck" than me. I even stopped wondering what my destiny was meant to be.

Instead, I started focusing on myself. I started focusing on my goals. I started looking for ways to get what I wanted in life. I started looking for ways to get to where I wanted to be. I started creating opportunities everywhere I went. I started absorbing as much as I could from my surroundings.

More importantly, I started taking action to create the life I had dreamed of.

If I was going to put my entire trust into myself, then I might as well be the best thing I could trust.

In the three years that have passed, I wasn't scared if I hit an obstacle. I knew I'd find a way to overcome it.

If something didn't go the way I had hoped, I trusted myself to find another way to get to where I wanted to be.

If I couldn't do something by myself, I trusted myself to find the right people to ask for help.

If I didn't know something, I trusted myself to learn it as I went along.

If there wasn't enough money to purchase something for my business, I trusted myself to find a more cost-effective way to accomplish the same goal.

That trust was powerful enough for me to believe that I could achieve whatever I desired. Not once in the last three years did I ever feel that I couldn't reach a specific goal or overcome any obstacle.

Because here's the thing:

The only person who can give you the life you want is **YOU.**

No other person can. You may think the circumstances are against you or that luck isn't on your side, but here's what I've begun to believe:

When you trust yourself, when you truly, relentlessly trust yourself, you start believing that you have the power to change your life.

You start believing that you have the power to change your destiny, your fate, or your luck.

When you start believing that, you stop trying to control everything around you, and instead, you focus on the one thing you can control—you. Once you learn to trust yourself regardless of the external circumstances, you feel more stable because you now have one thing you can count on. That's a powerful feeling, and it makes you confident to tackle anything that comes your way. Nothing will feel impossible anymore.

You also realize that the only reason you slipped and fell when the rug was pulled under you was because you were standing on it. You recognize that all you had to do in that moment was trust yourself to jump, and it wouldn't have mattered if the rug was being pulled or not.

Once you learn to control your actions, reactions, and thoughts, you automatically start aligning yourself to bring in the life you desire.

When you have the support of the most powerful thing in the world—*yourself*—what more could you ask for?

1.10

What makes you comfortable?

My parents are entrepreneurs themselves.

Since the age of thirteen, I have listened to stories of them running their own businesses during our dining table conversations. I consider myself highly privileged to have been privy to these conversations, to learn about the problems they were facing, what solutions they implemented, and how they managed their businesses. The discussions were very open.

As I grew older, we often had brainstorming sessions during our dinner. My dad would pose a problem, and we'd each give our thoughts on it. Not just that, we'd also talk about what would happen if we implemented each solution. I'm grateful to my parents for having these conversations in the open. They would always encourage my sister and me to think about what we would do if we had our own businesses. They made it a point to let us know our opinions mattered.

I remember when my parents were dejected because something didn't work out in their business. We'd order some ice cream, watch a movie together, and the next day I'd find my parents looking more determined than ever, ready to take on the problem with a fresh mindset.

I also remember their wins and how my parents would grin from ear to ear.

My sister and I would clap for them, and my dad would join in enthusiastically because he loved the chaos we brought! We still do it even today!

I saw how they overcame their struggles by finding better solutions. I understood their thought processes. I was in awe of their positive mindset. Their intense passion for making a difference with their businesses was something I also hoped to have in my life.

It was all very inspiring to me when I was growing up, and in many ways, the way they showed up for their businesses has shaped how I show up for my business today.

In May 2019, when I decided I wanted to start something on my own, it was safe to say I had a very, _very_ realistic view of how the journey was going to be.

I knew it was going to be rough. I knew it would take some time to see my efforts' results. I knew nine out of ten times I would be putting out fires.

But what shocked me was how much of it was on _me_ to do.

I don't just mean the tangible and obvious "work" part.

Yes, I had to create content.

Yes, I had to reach out to potential clients and discuss how I could help them.

Yes, I had to develop the products.

Yes, to all those things that you're pretty much aware you've got to do as a business owner.

I didn't realize the extent of intangible things that were on me.

Things like keeping my motivation up. Learning how to be self-disciplined. Knowing when to work. Remembering when I needed to take a break for my mental health. Understanding what I had to do right away and what I could push to a later date. Figuring out what I had to pursue and what I should walk away from. Setting deadlines for myself. Getting my work done within the deadline I had set for myself and so on.

All these decisions would throw me off. That was a bit of a cultural shock coming from a full-time job.

When you're working for someone, most of the time, the system is already in place for you. You have your manager outlining your tasks, your deadlines, etc. In most of these cases, you have a set time to start your work and a set time to end your work. The intangible decisions are already made for you. You have a defined set of tasks to bring a defined salary for the month.

The lack of structure can be very disorienting when you start working for yourself. It can also begin to get overwhelming because Every. Single. Thing. Is. On. You.

Of course, right after overwhelm, swoops in self-doubt, and you begin to doubt every single decision you make for your business.

You think you should wake up at 9 a.m., but then you see a video on YouTube that says all entrepreneurs need to wake up at 4 a.m. Then you start a new regime, but you realize your clients are on the other side of the world, and you need to stay up late, so the 4 a.m. thing doesn't work for you.

Then you hear someone saying they work fifteen hours a day, and you wonder if you're messing up your life by working twelve hours a day. Then someone else says they work only four hours a day, and again, you're confused about which advice or who to follow.

Soon, you realize there's no right way to go about this. That makes your decision process even harder.

You want to create your website and have unlimited time to do so. If you set the deadline too close, you will be super overwhelmed and won't be able to focus on anything else. If you set it too far away, you might forget about it.

So, what's the perfect spot?

This happens with *every* decision.

When should I stop feeling sad about the setback? When do I cut my losses for this product and move on to the next? When do I work on Task A? When should I finish Task A? When do I work on Task X? Is it before or after I finish Task A? When should I take a break? When should I get back to work? When do I acknowledge my burnout and take a vacation? How long do I go on a vacation?

There isn't anyone telling you if you're doing things right or not. There's no quarterly performance review that tells you where you are lacking and what you're excelling at.

There isn't anyone. It's just you. And let's face it, we're pretty biased when it comes to ourselves. We're either overly critical of ourselves or too lax. It's tough to strike a balance in the beginning.

Even as hyper-independent as I am, I was afraid to make a wrong decision. This put a lot of unnecessary pressure on me.

Over time of making countless intangible decisions for my business, here is one thing I learned:

The process involves a lot of trial and error, and that's okay.

As much as I'd like to give you a cookie-cutter solution to make the intangible decisions for your business, I've realized that there is no one way to make intangible decisions.

For example, when it comes to me, I need a day off at least once every week. I can work for three weeks without taking a break—and I have done that before during my product launches—but it always took a toll on my mental health. It was very hard for me to come out of the burnout, and after one such incident, I vowed that the maximum amount of time I'd work consecutively would be two weeks and nothing more than that.

I've seen entrepreneurs who can work for weeks without burning out, but that's not me. Given that most of my work is focused on being creative, I've realized I need that downtime to get my creativity flowing. I know my limitations, so I work around them.

That's just me. For you, you could need a break every three days. Or you could need a break every ten days.

Whatever it may be, it's not right or wrong. It's just a way that is suited to your needs and a way that makes *you* comfortable. It's easy to emulate people you are in awe of, but at the end of the day, you need to figure out what works for you.

The same goes for the other intangible decisions for your business. As much as possible, especially in the beginning, give yourself room to experiment with your choices.

It helps if you are open to trying different techniques and processes and tweaking them to match what works for you, your strengths, your weaknesses, your abilities, your skill set, etc.

Don't delay making the decisions, but at the same time, don't be too hard on yourself as you figure out what works for you.

A few questions you can ask yourself to get to know yourself better would be:

♦ Am I feeling comfortable with this method?

♦ By moving forward with this, am I unnecessarily complicating my life?

♦ Does this suit the kind of vision I have?

- Is there something that doesn't sit right with me when I try this?

- Am I doing it this way because I'm comfortable with it or because I feel pressured to follow in someone else's footsteps?

- What are my limitations, and how can I work around them?

- How can I take advantage of ___ (a strength)?

And remember, as your business grows, you'll have more intangible decisions to handle, but that mustn't faze you. As long as you're more open to trying ways that work for you, you'll navigate your business with better ease.

There may be no one way to make decisions, but it does help to find a way that works for you, doesn't it?

If you visit www.themarketingnomad.co/zero-to-four-figures, you'll get access to a printable workbook to understand yourself better.

1.11

All you need to do is bring your self-confidence higher than your self-doubt.

If I had a dollar for every time self-doubt crept up on me, I'd be writing a book on how I got to eight figures instead.

It is insane how self-doubt can catch you at any given moment. You've had your first loss; well, here comes self-doubt.

You've had your first win, and oh, look who is here—self-doubt.

You're minding your own business, going about your day, and poof, self-doubt appears.

You literally breathe, and what do ya know, self-doubt wants to be around.

I can distinctly remember times when I've written in my journal, wondering if I had it in me to achieve my dreams.

But I also remember that my next few sentences in my journal hushed my self-doubt into the corner of my mind and just focused on bringing my self-confidence to a point where it was more than my self-doubt. Even as I'm writing this book, it's not that I'm devoid of any self-doubt. Of course not.

I'm only human. There have been moments when I've paused my writing and wondered if I was in over my head with this. In fact, since I wrote this book to show other entrepreneurs and business owners that they weren't alone in their journey, let me give you an insight into what's running in my mind right now as I'm writing this book.

Thoughts in my head as of January 5, 2022, 11.57 a.m.:

Am I ever going to finish writing this book? Will people like it? What if they don't?

What if they can't connect with what I'm writing in this book? Have I bitten off more than I can chew?

No one's written a book about their business hitting four figures. What if there was a reason that they didn't, and the reason was that it was pointless?

And omg, marketing this book! That's an entirely different vertical in marketing. What if I fail in that? What is that going to say about me as a marketer?

Trust me, that's not even half of what's going on in my mind.

In April 2021, when my self-doubt was more than my self-confidence, I stopped writing this book. Instead of feeling bad about my self-doubt or trying to wipe it out completely, I decided to raise my self-confidence higher than my self-doubt.

I took a look at my composition book from Primary 3 and read through all the comments my teacher had written about my writing. She believed in my writing and always told me I had a unique talent. I also took the time to remember all the times when my essays were read out in class. I found the medal I received for winning first place in an essay writing competition back when I was sixteen. I took the time to raise my self-confidence. I kept growing it until it was greater than my self-doubt. I found this to be more straightforward than struggling to erase my self-doubt completely. I got back to writing the book in October 2021, once I raised my self-confidence to exceed my self-doubt.

Especially in the entrepreneurial world, I only hear people say, "You can't have self-doubt" or "Get out of your self-doubt."

While those are all excellent slogans, it's impossible to be without self-doubt. In fact, I think that's what's wrong with the way people think about self-doubt.

The reason people panic when they feel even a little bit of self-doubt is because there is a common perception that self-doubt needs to be eliminated entirely or that it shouldn't exist at all. They put all their focus on removing their self-doubt and are stuck trying to get it out of their system.

We fail to realize that it is normal for self-doubt to exist. I don't think there is anything wrong with self-doubt. It's usually a residue effect of a previous negative experience, and your mind is trying to safeguard you from repeating that experience again. Everyone goes through periods of self-doubt.

As long as your self-doubt doesn't exceed your self-confidence, you're doing okay. Instead of being stuck while you struggle to remove self-doubt, I'd like to share another way to help you move forward.

The simplest way to take the next step, especially when you have self-doubt, is to work your self-confidence to a point where it *exceeds* your self-doubt.

I believe that this journey is about moving forward, despite the self-doubt that exists. If I have to look back to when I started this entrepreneurial journey, or when I decided to set up my company, or even during my product launches, I had self-doubt. But I took actionable steps to raise my self-confidence more than my self-doubt, which helped me take the next step.

On this journey, you'll find yourself struggling with self-doubt. A lot. It is entirely natural, and there is nothing to be ashamed of. Your self-doubt exists to help you show up better. For example, because of my tiny bit of self-doubt with marketing my book, I will be triple checking the marketing strategies I lay out. Regarding my self-doubt when it comes to my writing, I've deleted a quarter of what I intended to write because it didn't meet my standards. My self-doubt did help me be absolutely sure of what I wanted to write in this book.

If you ask me, I think a healthy amount of self-doubt is necessary. As long as it isn't hindering you from taking your next step, it's okay that it exists. If it does come to a point where it restricts you from taking your next step, find actionable steps to get your self-confidence higher than your self-doubt.

You can do that by asking yourself these questions:

♦   Why do I feel self-doubt?

♦   Is my self-doubt protecting me or hindering me?

♦   If it hinders me, what steps can I take to raise my self-confidence? *(This could be taking a course, doing more research, reminding yourself of your past achievements/awards, etc.)*

Once your self-confidence exceeds your self-doubt, you'll automatically feel ready to move forward. You'll acknowledge that your self-doubt is in a tiny corner of your mind, but it isn't stopping you.

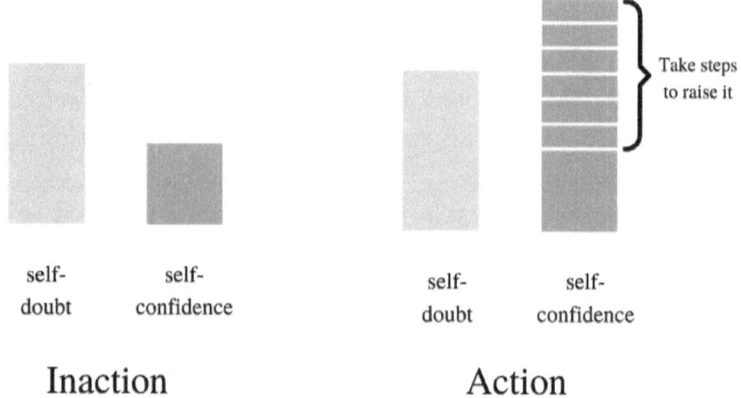

Another thing about self-doubt is that it reduces as you find more proof that you can do the task on hand, which means your self-doubt only reduces *after* you've completed the task and found success with it. That success reaffirms you can do the task, so when you do the same thing the next time, you're working with less self-doubt.

You can try to erase your self-doubt while you're working through your task, but it is much more complicated than if you were to work on raising your self-confidence instead.

In the game of self-doubt vs. self-confidence, it's about ensuring self-confidence has more points than self-doubt.

After all, we all want self-confidence to win, right?

1.12

Give yourself space and time to recognize your passion.

When I was in my second year of engineering, I was sure about one thing: engineering was not something I saw myself doing for the next forty years of my life.

For a twenty-year-old, that was a scary thought. Most of my classmates seemed to like engineering. They were in their element, and here I was, feeling like a fish out of water.

It wasn't that I didn't find my field interesting. I did. Being naturally curious, I was interested to know more about how everything around me worked. I just wasn't feeling passionate about it.

All my life, I had been intensely passionate about dancing, and I yearned to feel the same about something I would be doing for a significant chunk of my life.

As the second year of my engineering went on, I found myself feeling more lost. This was in 2012, and at the time, there was a lot of prejudice when it came to pursuing one's passion.

If you were anything other than an Engineer, Doctor, or Lawyer, people couldn't bring themselves to respect you. And if someone did manage to fight the odds to pursue something they were passionate about, it was always met with huge amounts of skepticism and people writing them off as a destined failure. If you managed to find success, it was almost always written off as "sheer, dumb luck".

So, there I was, struggling to make my passion magically appear. I'd be staring into my textbook, closing my eyes, hoping there would be a change in the way I felt about engineering as I counted, "One, two aaaaandddd three!"

You guessed it; it did not.

During my summer holidays, my father, in a typical Indian parent style, said I should try to find an internship instead of lazing around. I scoffed and said no one would give me an internship with the kind of marks I had.

My dad laughed out loud but quickly covered it as a cough as he caught my mother's raised eyebrow.

So, the next day, my dad took me to his office. I went grumpily. What was I going to do there? I didn't remember anything I had studied, and I really didn't want to have anything to do with engineering.

I sat in my dad's office as he went to bring one of his employees. I fiddled with a black Mont Blanc pen that was on the table. I accidentally dropped the pen cap on the floor, and it went right under the inaccessible part of the table. I promptly put the pen back and pretended it always existed without a cap. Legend says the pen cap still exists under the table to this day.

Anyway, my dad introduced one of his employees and asked me to help them with the company website. My job was simple. I had to look at their website and point out any mistakes so his website team could correct them.

I went through each page. Made note of the grammatical mistakes and the spelling errors.

Then there was one sentence that I rephrased. I thought my version of the sentence communicated the message better. There was another page where the color scheme wasn't aligned with the website's overall aesthetic. I made a note of that too.

After helping with the website, I went on to help them with their Facebook page. Given my flair for writing, I helped them with the captions. I monitored the company's growth on its social media pages. I observed the kind of content their audience liked and let the social media team know which types of posts to upload.

I would come to realize years later that all that I was doing was a part of marketing. At the time, I really had no idea what it was called.

I enjoyed my time at my dad's company. Time flew. I didn't know how I was able to piece things together in my head, but somewhere up there, my thoughts just flowed. I even returned the next two summers voluntarily and enthusiastically to help my dad's company with its online presence.

It was also around this time that I got involved in organizing my engineering college's annual fest. I organized a flash mob every year and was a part of the outreach team.

I don't know how and why my mind was so fast in strategizing for these events, but I absolutely loved every minute of it. I felt my passion firing up, and I'd immediately feel sad because I had no idea how I'd go from being an engineer to becoming someone who did all of these different things. I mean, what even was all of this? Did people get paid for this stuff? I didn't have any answers then; rather, I never tried to find answers to those questions. I just didn't think it was a possibility for me.

By my last year of engineering, I started to look at other alternatives. I was very sure that I did not want to pursue a career in engineering. I did not even apply for a single job. After listening to my parents talk about their businesses during my teens, I knew I would start my own business someday.

So, I decided to do an MBA after getting my engineering degree. This was my only plan, and I didn't have any fallback option. I was overjoyed when I got my acceptance letter from a good university in Rochester, New York!

Fast forward to my first marketing class. The professor was asking a few questions just to engage the class, and there I was, answering every question. I remembered a Coca-cola marketing campaign from ten years ago and explained the campaign in detail. I remembered a Maggi marketing campaign from three years ago and spoke about what fascinated me about it.

I was so surprised! Turns out that all my life, my mind had been absorbing little bits of information about marketing. I liked reading about it; without my knowledge, I would try to know as much as possible about it.

That moment, sitting in my first marketing class, was a turning point in my life and career. It felt like my entire life had led to this moment. I had finally recognized my passion. After four long years of confusion and despair, I knew this was a precious feeling. I promised myself I would never take my love for marketing for granted.

I wanted to share this story with you because some of you reading this book may not have found your passion yet. For those of us who have envisioned taking the entrepreneurial route someday, we're instinctively driven to find something we are passionate about. It can be a bit scary when you're moving through life, unable to find your passion while everyone around you has their life seemingly figured out.

But here's the thing:

Passion isn't something that is found.

Passion isn't something that shows up one day on your doorstep.

Passion isn't something that you wake one day and feel it.

It already exists within you. It's in little bits of actions that you've taken since the beginning of your life. Passion is cultivated within you over years and years, and it is so powerful that sometimes, it grows without you realizing it even exists. You've just got to give yourself some space and time to recognize it.

If you're feeling a bit lost about not recognizing your passion in life yet, then I wish to tell you this:

So many people live their entire lives without a second thought about finding something they are passionate about. Others don't allow themselves to dream of a life filled with passion. The fact that you know you want a different kind of life, a life with passion, puts you at the starting point of getting your life figured out. While people around you may seem farther along in their life, you must understand that your track is entirely different from theirs, so how can you expect your life's timelines to match what other people perceive as "normal"?

When you recognize you want something more out of life, it will also help you to realize your passion. The more you try to find it, the more frustrated you will be, and frustration is usually on the opposite side of passion. How can you expect to recognize your passion when you are closed off with fear and frustration?

So, take a deep breath, yes, right now, as you're holding this book in your hand. Take a deep breath and look back at the actions you've taken in your life so far.

What do you find yourself doing that makes you unimaginably happy?

Is there something that you immerse yourself in, but maybe you haven't thought about making a career out of it?

Take some time to reflect. The answer lies within you and the life that you have led till now. You will recognize it, I promise.

Now I know this lesson may not resonate with everyone. Some people reading this book may have already found their passion. This particular lesson is for those who want to lead a career path that they are passionate about but are worried that they haven't figured it out yet. I wrote this because if there is only one thing I could go back in time and tell my twenty-year-old self, it would be this very lesson. I really, *really* wish I had read this during that phase of my life, and I know there may be someone out there who needs to hear this as well. I hope my story of recognizing my passion gives you hope that you will too.

For those of you who have found your passion, I do have a tiny message for you too: If you're one of the lucky ones to have found something that you are passionate about, something that really lights your soul on fire and gives you a sense of purpose, don't let that go to waste. Very few people find that kind of passion in their lives, and we owe it to ourselves to see where it can take us.

We may have different origin stories, but isn't it amazing that our quest for a life of passion is what unites us all?

CHAPTER 2
POSITIVE MINDSET

Be realistic ✔

Face challenges ✔

Don't die ✔

Your outlook matters the most.

If you're not happy where you are, a bold step is all it takes to change it.

One question I get asked a lot from my friends is if I regret getting my engineering degree.

You see, I've switched my career path since then, so to them, it looks like I wasted a few years of my life getting a degree in engineering.

However, I don't feel that way at all. Even though I didn't see myself having a career in engineering, I will never regret the time I spent getting the degree, and here's why:

One perk about having an engineering degree is that the time you spend getting that degree teaches you a new way to view life. Fundamentally, engineers are problem solvers.

During the entire course of an engineering degree, we're taught to figure out what the problem is. Not just that, we're taught how to look for the root of the problem.

You could find the root through trial and error, applying logic, or using various formulae.

Once we figure out the problem, we're trained to find creative solutions. After repeating this process over time, we subconsciously apply it to other issues in our life.

You will never find an engineer who doesn't sprout solutions the minute you say you have a problem. When we, and by we, I mean engineers, hear the word "problem", our brain goes into overdrive, and we immediately start to come up with various possibilities to solve it.

The degree just wires you that way.

My mom, an engineer herself, always told me that engineering is a way of life, and frankly, I think that's true.

Now in May 2019, I was unhappy for quite some time. I soon started feeling irritated with how long I was unhappy.

That was odd.

So now I had to process two emotions. One was unhappiness and the other irritation.

The feeling of being overwhelmed caught up with my two existing emotions, and soon I had to process *three* emotions.

Anxiety didn't want to feel out of the loop, so it too joined the party.

Fear wasn't far behind either.

Instead of trying to process one emotion in peace, I now had to work through a whole horde of emotions.

These emotions started sticking to me like glue, and it was getting harder for me to brush them off.

So naturally, when all these emotions were piling on, the engineer in me realized I had a problem on hand.

My first step was to analyze the root of the problem. The first emotion that even began this whole downward spiral was my unhappiness.

Even if I could somehow remove each of those emotions one by one, it wouldn't change the fact that I was unhappy.

My next step was to find as many solutions as possible.

I danced to my favorite Bollywood music for thirty minutes. I thought maybe if I did it every day, I'd somehow trick myself into being happy.

I forgot my unhappiness for those few minutes, but when I turned off the music because I was grossly out of breath, my unhappiness hit me even harder.

I tried cooking my favorite food. I cried while eating it because I remembered my days of cooking in my cute little kitchen on Long Island were numbered.

So no, that did not work either.

I soon realized that the solutions I was trying were not helping me eliminate my unhappiness. These solutions were only helping me ignore it temporarily.

At this point, I had a conversation with myself:

"Alrighty Prit, where are you right now?"

"I'm unhappy."

"Where do you want to be?"

"I don't know; I just want to feel happy again."

"So, you want to be happy?"

"Yes."

"But you are unhappy right now."

"Yes."

"But you want to be happy."

"YES, HOW MANY TIMES DO I SAY THAT?"

silence

"I'm sorry. That was uncalled for."

"It's okay; you're doing your best."

"Thanks. You get me."

"...Ohhhkay, so where were we? You're at Point A; you want to get to Point B. How do you get to Point B?"

"I must leave Point A by stepping towards Point B."

"There you go."

And it hit me. I had to take a step. Not just any step, but a step that would help me leave Point A, *and* that was in the direction of Point B.

It had been a few days since I'd met the three entrepreneurs. If Point B was starting my own business and finding some sort of happiness there, then my next step would be to call them up and ask them about their journey.

I thought it would be weird. I mean, how would I even go about it? What would they think of me?

I mulled over it for an hour. I was desperate to get out of Point A. That was enough for me to stop caring about what they would think about me.

I reached out to them, which was the first step to starting my own business.

It took courage.

It took strength.

It took me being open-minded.

First, I had to understand that I could change my state of being and that I didn't have to stay in my current state forever.

I also realized that no one was going to get me out of my unhappy state. No one else was going to get me to take the first step.

Only *I* could take that bold step.

I felt considerably happier. I now had a plan. I had a tiny vision to work towards. I found joy in teaching myself new things to set up my business. I was working away on my laptop, shopping for domain names, setting up my website, and... get this, I was smiling to myself!

Taking that one bold step made me realize I was already at Point B.

Very often, when we think of the life we want, it can feel really far away. We may think that it takes many, many steps to get there. That can leave us confused and scared, thus not taking a single step.

But here's a little secret: All it takes is one bold step to live the life that makes you happy.

Our heart's desire and happiness lie on the other side of fear; all it takes are those few moments of bravery and courage to take a bold step towards it.

You can accept that you are unhappy, but that doesn't mean you have to stay in that state. There is only one step between Point A and Point B.

Life is about moving past the fear and having the courage to make the bold step to change your state of being.

The bold step to start something on your own.

The bold step to submit a proposal for a freelance project.

The bold step to show up on social media for your business.

There's no ridiculous number of steps that exhaust you by just looking at it.

One bold step to unlock the life you've always wished for. Question is, what's your bold step going to be?

2.2

If you wanted a simpler life, you should have had a simpler goal.

My late teens and early twenties were turbulent.

Most of my troubles were from my own doing, be it involving myself in toxic personal relationships or acting out because I was frustrated with the lack of direction in my life. I'm comfortable admitting this now, though back then, I just blamed everything else.

That had been my mindset for a long time—the "victim" mentality, as many people would call it. I would always blame external circumstances, fate, or anything else to suggest that it wasn't my doing. In fact, I think I liked blaming everything else because that meant evading the responsibility of my life.

Now let me tell you the story of how I began to accept that my life was my doing and my doing alone.

I've always wanted to own a business.

Growing up, during my family's dining table conversations, I'd always hear my parents talk about their mysterious "bosses" and how my parents had to follow their instructions.

That was interesting to me as a seven-year-old. As a kid who always had to listen to my parents, it was funny that there was someone my parents had to listen *to*.

I mean, I had to listen to how my parents wanted me to behave, what was right, what was wrong. I even had to listen to them when they said I couldn't miss school without a valid reason! *(It might be helpful for me to mention I was a bit of a rebel.)*

But when I realized my parents had to listen to someone else, their "boss", to be precise, my mind started racing. If *I* could become the boss, my parents might listen to *me* instead.

When I asked my parents what this "boss" of theirs did, they said they were the head of the company, sort of like the principal of my school. They explained that just like I had to listen to my teachers, my teachers had to listen to the principal. Turns out my parents were like the teachers while their respective bosses were like the principal of the school.

After hearing this, I liked the idea of becoming a boss much more.

So, as a kid, while my friends wanted to be doctors or engineers, I always *knew* I would start my own company someday. In every single class project, I would take on the leadership role and feel important while making decisions for the direction of those projects.

"The Boss. That's who I'm going to be." – Prithvi Madhukar, Aged 7.

Did I know what being a "boss" even meant? Nope, of course not. I knew it meant I was doing some serious work, people would listen to me *(more importantly, my parents)*, and I would be the company's project leader. So, a company leader essentially.

As I grew older and started to understand the business world a little more, I did not waiver from my resolution. Of course, it wasn't because of the same reasons I had when I was seven. By this time, I was sure I wanted to make a difference to the people around me, and I knew the best way I could do that was to start something on my own. I wasn't sure how I'd get there, but I secretly gave myself a deadline to be a CEO by the age of twenty-seven. I don't know how or why I picked twenty-seven, but it was a solemn promise I made to myself when I was sixteen.

In my early twenties, I studied to get an engineering degree. Unfortunately, it wasn't a field that made me happy. That made me feel scared and anxious about my future because I thought I was supposed to have my life figured out by this time.

Somewhere during my engineering days, I was so focused on figuring out what I wanted to do with my life that my dream of starting my own company faded.

How could I start my own company when I hadn't chosen a field to work in? Or even find one that I was remotely passionate about?

No, that didn't seem right.

I was twenty-one years old then, and to have my life figured out *and* start a company by the age of twenty-seven seemed impossible.

So, I let go of the deadline I had promised myself and instead felt convinced I could still start something on my own when I was in my mid-thirties. I would have figured my life out by then, I comforted myself.

I was twenty-four when I found my love and passion for marketing during my master's degree. It was a happy surprise for me. During this time, I also met a lot of international students who were pursuing their master's degrees. Their plan was to get a job in the US, work there for a while, settle down, get a green card, and eventually get their citizenship.

Good plan, I thought to myself. I decided to have that exact plan too.

I continued living according to the new plan that matched everyone around me. I had finally found my career path. I wanted to keep hanging on to the certainty. I was no longer an odd duck. I was finally going to be a part of a larger crowd who had planned their life out, and I didn't want to do anything to jeopardize that.

I figured I would get into the entrepreneurial world five or maybe ten years later. Until then, I would get my degree, work full-time in the US, and live the normal life everyone else dreamed of.

Fast forward to a lazy Sunday afternoon in June 2019, where I was sitting on my bed, looking for domain names, sure of taking a leap into the entrepreneurial world. As I was thinking of how I wanted to structure the "About Me" section on my website, it triggered a flashback to the declaration I had made when I was a little girl. I chuckled at how a week ago, the thought of being an entrepreneur had not even crossed my mind, and here I was, setting up my platforms as a freelancer.

My life's events led me to this moment.

Here's what the Universe (or higher power, whichever you believe in) is about: it doesn't forget the intentions you set. It especially doesn't forget the ones you wished for with all your heart.

My intention of becoming a CEO by the age of twenty-seven was already set in stone. The life I had led up until then was only taking me to the end goal I had set.

Let me reiterate that.

Who had set the intention? Me.

Who had a secret dream? Me.

Who had a goal in mind? Me.

Who was responsible for the journey that was leading me to my goal?

Yes, it was me.

Though I admit, I answered the last question begrudgingly.

I also realized I was only copying everyone else's dream of leading the kind of life *they* wanted. I was so afraid to stand out that I had let go of my own dreams to start something on my own. But deep down, it was something I really wanted to do, and I did want to do it by twenty-seven, even though I couldn't admit it.

Because of my continued intention, everything fell into place at the intended time.

I'll give you another example. I knew I would be an author someday. When I wrote my first composition in Primary 1, my teacher said I had a talent for writing and should keep working on it. Throughout my education, my English teachers always affirmed that they saw something magical in my writing. Everyone praising my writing made me more confident, and that led me to believe I would write a book someday.

Again, if I didn't have a life I could write about for a non-fiction book or hadn't been through the stuff that I did go through to extrapolate it into a fiction book, I think writing would have been the last thing on my mind.

As painful as the downs in my life were, they had one goal in mind:

To get me to where I said I wanted to be.

This was a powerful realization for me. So powerful that I had to pause from my domain name shopping and reflect on every single moment in my life that had led me right to that moment. If I had changed even one decision or skipped going through any one of my lows, I wouldn't have arrived where I said I wanted to be.

I was responsible for the life I had led and the life yet to unfold.

The minute I realized I was responsible for my life's ups *and* downs; it jolted me out of the victim mentality. I started to take responsibility for every moment of my life that had occurred and those yet to come.

If I wanted a simpler life, I should have chosen a simpler goal.

But that's the thing. I've *never* wanted an ordinary life. Even as a kid, I strived to be apart from the rest.

It was illogical of me to want an extraordinary life then not go through all the things that helped to make it extraordinary.

How could I complain when every incident in my life had to be experienced by me so I could create the life I wanted?

I couldn't. I really couldn't complain.

When you choose the entrepreneurship path, you must realize that **YOU** are the person making the decision. That means the only person responsible for everything that happens to get you there and what happens after is on you.

Not on life. Not on fate. Not on your annoying neighbor Tom, and not on luck.

The more you accept that you are responsible for your life, the easier it will be for you to cope and make peace with the lows that come with this journey. You also start to trust that whatever is happening, regardless of how sad it may make you feel in the moment, is happening to bring your innermost desires into reality.

From this moment, I started to feel that life wasn't against me. Everything that was happening allowed me to realize the life I truly wanted.

Even today, if something is challenging or I'm facing a low, it makes me sad or frustrated. But, at the same time, I trust that this needs to happen so it can all come together in the best way.

If you wanted a simpler life, you should have chosen a simpler goal.

The life you lead is always correlated to the goals you set for yourself. If you'd like to achieve a more challenging goal, then the kind of experiences that you face will align to help you get there.

It will be harder.

It will be more painful.

It will be steeper.

But that's on you to choose the goal.

You choose the journey, and of course, you have free will to opt-out of the journey as well. But what you can't do is continue to choose a more demanding goal and then complain about the experiences you must go through to get you to the endpoint you desire.

So, what would you like in your experience today—An easier or harder goal?

2.3

Learn to embrace change.

Upon realizing my work visa would not be processed, I didn't think I would ever feel happy again.

I was not being dramatic. I really felt that way. Life had knocked me down before, but in all those times, I knew I'd go back to being happy.

This time, it was different. It was hard for me to believe that any outcome from this would ever compare to the life I had envisioned for myself in New York.

Something about me: I've always felt a strong bond with butterflies. Seeing butterflies makes me believe something beautiful is on its way into my life. Over the years, it's become more evident that the butterfly is my spirit animal.

When I look back, my life has been a series of distinct phases, each leading to a massive transformation in me, to a point where the people who've known me in each of these phases had to relearn the person I am today.

My life has broken down entirely in every phase and been remade from scratch. That has taught me how to gracefully navigate through extreme life changes.

So, in May 2019, when this feeling of despair started to snowball, I realized it was time for me to remember how I had coped with the previous significant changes in my life.

Step 1: Take Time to Process Your Emotions

I think it's clear that I was a mess of all possible emotions at this point.

I was sad. I was angry. I was frustrated. I was anxious. I was jealous.

I was also looking down on myself for having all of these emotions. I didn't want to be so emotional and look weak in front of everyone.

I suppressed my emotions a lot during this time. When I would meet my friends, I would pretend I was okay and that I had entirely accepted my fate.

Doing this invariably led me to become more emotional. Since I wasn't processing my emotions, they were getting complex as the days passed.

Soon, it was hard for me to even discern what emotions I was feeling. That's when I knew I had messed up. I knew I had to face them someday. To accept my feelings, I had to learn that it was okay and natural for me to feel this way. I had to accept that I was only human.

Because I could not understand my complex emotions anymore, I started writing my thoughts on paper. At the time, I didn't call it journaling. I just took a blank piece of paper and started writing everything I felt. I didn't stop writing even when my right hand started to ache. Sometimes the thoughts in my mind were running faster than the speed I could write, but even then, I didn't give up. I just kept going.

After I had written everything I was feeling, I took a break. I took out the trash. I went out to get groceries for dinner. I mindlessly went about my day.

The next day, I gingerly picked up those sheets of paper I had written on. Now that they were all on paper, they seemed tangible, which scared me a little. Would I like what I was about to read? What if reading my thoughts had an adverse effect? I brushed these thoughts, took a deep breath, and my eyes rested on the first line.

It felt like I was reading someone else's thoughts instead of mine. It seemed like I was peering on the other side of the glass, watching someone else's life unfold. All the emotions on those papers seemed valid. As I read through those papers, I didn't feel any of those emotions were unnecessary or ridiculous.

I took a different color pen and started writing my counter-thoughts on each sentence. I gave some words of encouragement on the side. I analyzed every emotion that was mentioned. I even wrote ways to overcome those feelings. The best part about this was I fully and wholly accepted myself.

This helped me take the next step to remind myself that it was okay to feel what I was feeling.

When you're going through a rough time, it's easier to brush off your emotions or to be angry with yourself for having those emotions. The more you berate yourself for feeling, the more complex those emotions start to get. As they get more complex, it becomes harder to find a way out of feeling those emotions. This part of the process is crucial because you learn how to look at your situation objectively, and in turn, this helps you see your next steps clearly.

For me, writing my emotions on paper helped me process them. For you, it could be something else. I've met people who processed their emotions with a video diary by recording themselves thinking aloud and revisiting it later. My point is that it doesn't matter how you process your emotions as long as you invest time to do it. What's important is that you find a way that works for you.

Basically, if you're feeling sad, accept it. If you're angry, again, feel it in its entirety. Lean into what you're feeling instead of suppressing it.

One of the most important things about this step is to recognize that your feelings are valid, and you don't need to justify what you are feeling.

In my experience, the more you understand what you're feeling, the more you accept it. The more you can accept what you feel, the easier it is to find a starting point to work through it.

Step 2: Embrace the Uncertainty

Another step in my entire process was to embrace the uncertainty. That wasn't as easy as it sounded. I didn't know what my life would look like two months from then.

Every other minute, my mind was spinning with questions. What was I supposed to do next? How was I going to deal with this? How would I face people after this?

Each time those questions plagued me, it would be full-blown anxiety attacks with me slumping to the floor and crying.

It was around this time that I remembered something from sixth grade.

We had yoga sessions in my school. Our yoga teacher would make us do mediation for a few minutes every Wednesday.

I absolutely hated it.

My mind could never stay calm. There were always thoughts running, and I never understood the concept of having no thoughts. It wasn't possible for me, and there was no way I was going to force myself to do it.

In ninth and tenth grade, I had a teacher who would make us meditate for five minutes before starting our day. I'd just close my eyes for the heck of it, but I never felt any "enlightenment" from it, nor did I feel there was any difference after. After tenth grade, I never once thought about meditation. When people mentioned meditation, I would laugh and say that my mind was way too complex to be calmed by meditation.

I don't know how I remembered this whole meditation thing, but I thought it would be worth a try.

I searched for some meditation music on YouTube and played it.[4] I lay on my bed, took a deep breath, and closed my eyes.

Whatisgoingtohappenhowamigoingtodealwiththisthisisnotworkingitisntwor kidontthinksothisissoweirdamiwastingmytime with this am I ever g o i n g t o f e e l b e t t e r

Within thirty minutes, I could feel my thoughts spacing out. What was going at 300 miles per hour in my mind was now going at half the rate.

I slept well that night.

The next day, I woke up feeling lighter. Not entirely, but there was enough difference for me to try meditation again. And then I did it the next day. And then the next.

With each passing day, I could feel myself becoming more present. I even caught myself laughing at a memory when I was packing the things in my studio apartment.

The calmer my mind became, the sillier it felt that I needed to have all the answers.

"Not even my parents have all the answers!" I declared one day, brimming with confidence.

Each time I would wonder about what was coming ahead, I found myself saying, *"I don't know, and that's okay."*

Whenever I would ask myself how I would face the whole situation, I'd surprise myself by saying, *"Let's deal with today first."*

I decided to try guided meditations too, which helped me become more confident in myself.

---

[4] I listened to Jason Stephenson on YouTube. Highly recommend this channel for meditation music: https://www.youtube.com/c/JasonStephensonSleepMeditationMusic

There are so many things about the subconscious mind that we may not understand, but I have to say, meditation unlocked my inner strength.

As I'm writing this book and reflecting, I am ashamed of all those times I was naïve and took meditation for granted. In many ways, it saved me, and I am forever grateful for it.

I've made meditation a priority in the last three years of my entrepreneurial journey. Each time I've felt myself panicking or my anxiety rising, I've taken a step back and gotten to my normal state with the help of meditation.

I have come to realize that meditation isn't about having no thoughts. To me, and this will vary for each person, meditation is the time I give myself to slow down and look at what's running in my mind. It's that time of the day when I don't judge my thoughts but instead watch them flow.

I don't stop thoughts from flowing in my mind; instead, during my meditation, I give them a direction to flow in. That automatically puts me in a calmer mode.

When you are running your own business, every next moment is uncertain. Either you're working to solve problems or figuring out how to sustain something that's going right. There are tons of thoughts that will constantly be circling in your mind.

It helps to meditate. You can call it meditation, or you can call it giving yourself time to relax, or it could even just be a way for you to be by yourself in silence for a few moments.

I have found this to be one of the best practices to cope with all the pressures and uncertainties of running one's own business.

Step 3: Find Ways to Accept What Is

When it comes to significant life changes, most of the time, you feel unbalanced because it no longer aligns with what you had hoped for or how you envisioned things to go.

The same happened when I realized my H-1B work visa had not been processed. My reality was now significantly different from the vision I had of my life previously.

I was no longer going to be at the job I loved. I was no longer going to be working with my colleagues. My best friends and I would no longer be in the same country, let alone the same city.

That was heartbreaking.

The reason why I was unable to cope with the situation was because I couldn't accept my new reality. There was a considerable gap between where I thought my life would go and where my life was headed. I could not bridge that gap, causing me a lot of pain.

After returning to India and living my new version, I slowly started accepting my new life. I began to bridge the gap by accepting where I was currently.

I was in India. I was living with my parents and sister. I was now a digital entrepreneur. A person who had to FaceTime her best friends.

I accepted this new life. It wasn't until December 2019 that I fully made peace with where I was. I didn't consciously do this, but when I realized I had made peace with my new life, I knew it was instrumental to my healing process.

On many occasions, you will find yourself very frustrated about how slow things are moving for your business. Sometimes, you might even find yourself unaware of a sudden change and feel confused about how to process the changes. In times like that, I've found that when we start to work from where we *are*, instead of where we hoped for, the cloud clears, we begin to see the positives, and slowly, we find happiness.

And that's the goal, isn't it?

2.4

The simplest way to get what you want is to first walk away from the things that bring you what you don't want.

While I was growing up in Singapore, we lived near the East Coast Park.[5]

The East Coast Park is the largest park in Singapore, and it is built on reclaimed land. It even has a man-made beach with its own barbeque pits and local hawker center stalls with delicious food.

We lived about ten minutes away by bus and would visit East Coast Park at least once a month.

Sometimes my parents and their friends would plan Barbeque Sundays with each family bringing a dish for the potluck. My mom would prepare spaghetti, Bee Hoon, or Lemon Rice and pack it into a big box. She would also add some spoons, paper cups, paper towels, and some paper plates for the picnic.

The adults would find a nice spot to set up and place all their items on the table, giving the children some standard instructions so we would be careful. After half an hour of frolicking in the water, I'd get bored. I would run to

---

[5] *East Coast Park.* (2022). National Parks Board. https://www.nparks.gov.sg/gardens-parks-and-nature/parks-and-nature-reserves/east-coast-park

my mom, asking if I could collect some seashells and pebbles instead. I've always been fascinated with pebbles, and I have no idea why, but let's just roll with it.

I wasn't allowed to take them home because, according to my mom, *"I never made use of them"* and all they did was *"gather dust"*. Unfortunately, this was true.

Previously I would convince her that I'd use the pebbles and seashells for an upcoming art project. However, after I got back home, I would forget about them. I would also leave them lying around the house and as we know, that is every mom's pet peeve.

So, as a result of my actions, I was allowed to collect them, but I had to leave them behind.

After getting permission to collect seashells and pebbles, I'd ask my mom for something to put them into.

My mom would pause mid-conversation with her friends, look around the table, and find a paper cup for me. Sometimes the paper cup had a little bit of trash, so she'd ask me to throw the trash into a dustbin near our spot, rinse the paper cup with the cool, blueish-green beach water, and then use it to collect whatever I wanted.

One time, I felt lazy and ignored throwing out the little bits of trash from the paper cup. I went ahead to collect those pebbles and seashells. Either way, I was going to put the pebbles and seashells back, so I figured there was no point in cleaning out the paper cup.

However, something felt different this time. Every time I'd look in the paper cup, I could see those seashells, but I'd also see the trash.

I could swear that the trash that looked small before I started collecting, had grown twice its size and stood out more awkwardly in contrast to the seashells. It wasn't as satisfying as looking at a paper cup filled with only seashells. A funky smell would also come out of the paper cup, which would make me realize my mom was right.

From then on, I always took the time to remove the trash from the paper cup first before collecting my seashells and pebbles.

As I grew older, I started to equate the lesson I had learned to my life.

In life, we each get a paper cup to fill whatever we want to. Most of the time, we ignore the existing trash and continue to add the things that bring us what we want. After a while, each time you look at your cup, even though you see the items you want, what catches your eye more are the things you don't want.

Over time, the trash becomes more prominent, and you tend to focus only on it.

Each time you look at your cup, you don't feel accomplished. Instead of focusing on the positive things in your cup, you become dejected at the seemingly huge negative stuff in your cup.

Each time you look in your cup, it doesn't make you feel good, so you stop looking at your cup.

At some point, you forget that you even had a cup to begin with.

That's when the negative self-thought happens. You start to forget that you can have what you want. You begin to forget that you, and only you, control what goes into your cup.

All of this could be avoided if you simply took the time to remove the trash from the paper cup first.

Let's apply this concept to growing a business:

If you want to grow your business, the first step you need to take is to walk away from the things that keep your business stagnant, regardless of how enticing they may be.

That includes your mindset.

When I started my journey, I had to let go of every thought that brought me what I did not want. These were thoughts of doubt, imposter syndrome, or my worry about having a successful career. I also had to let go of the people who would not allow me to have the peace of mind I needed to run my business.

If I recall how I achieved every single one of my goals up until now, it all began with walking away from something that did not serve me.

When I started my own Etsy digital shop in December 2020, I was already a YouTuber, Membership Owner, Podcaster, and Marketing Consultant. My time was already spread thin across different platforms.

I knew that if I wanted to succeed with my Etsy digital shop, I needed to take a hard look at what was serving me and what wasn't.

It took some time to decide to end my membership program, but I did it. It wasn't bringing the return on investment I was hoping for, and I just wasn't happy. It was hard to walk away from it because that was literally one year's worth of time and effort on my end.

After walking away from it, I had the time and capacity to focus on my Etsy digital shop. I was able to dedicate a lot of time to doing my research and creating the exact kind of products my audience needed. Over time, I began to see myself hitting milestones after milestones for my Etsy digital shop. In an email from Etsy on March 18, 2022, I was awarded a "Star Seller" on Etsy for six consecutive months, and according to the email, I was one in 0.5% of their 5.6 million sellers to get that recognition!

The best part? I absolutely enjoy every minute of building my digital shop.

I wouldn't have been able to achieve this success if I hadn't walked away from the things that brought me what I didn't want.

When you recognize what you want, it is natural to move towards it.

You want to have a successful relationship, so you move towards finding the right partner for you.

You want to grow a successful business, so you move towards creating processes and systems that will help you achieve that.

In our rush to start moving towards what we want, we often forget that if you want something in life, you must first have the courage to walk away from the things that bring you what you don't want.

For example—the courage to walk away from our co-dependency patterns so we can move towards a healthy relationship. Or the courage to first walk away from processes that no longer serve us so we can build a business that can sustain long-term.

Without doing the first and most crucial step, it's harder to get what you want.

You can still get what you want without this step, of course, but there's going to be a lousy aftertaste to the entire experience, or something just won't feel right after you get what you want.

So, the simplest and most enjoyable way to get what we want is to make sure we take the time to empty our cups before we start filling them with the things we want.

Isn't the most enjoyable way the best way to get what we want?

2.5

If they're wasting their time judging you, that's on them. If you're wasting your time worrying about it, that's on you.

Around October 2019, I talked to an old friend, and everything seemed fine until I heard them say, "So *you're* going to be an entrepreneur?" and they snickered.

I was a bit stumped. They meant to pose it as a joke, but it was clear that they were judging me for the decision I had made. I had known them since I was sixteen, and it was hurtful that someone who had known me for that long was judging me.

It didn't stop there. Every time I tried something new for my business, I had at least one person judging me.

In September 2020, I started talking more about my struggles as an entrepreneur and business owner. I hoped business owners listening to my struggles would know they weren't alone on this journey. Someone who knew me from childhood asked me why I was being a drama queen because I was sharing the ups and downs of my journey. Yeah, go figure.

I started my YouTube channel, and I had someone reach out to me to say that they thought I just wanted attention.

I started my Etsy digital shop, and someone mockingly said they imagined me making my own jewelry and selling it. I honestly didn't see the point in being judgmental about making one's jewelry and selling it on Etsy. I've seen so many successful sellers on Etsy who earn a very comfortable income from Etsy by creating and selling their jewelry. I didn't get the point of their snub, but that's just the reality of some people's perception.

It would bother me at first, but I realized that I was just wasting my time worrying about them judging me.

Even though I've stopped caring, I'll be honest, there are unconventional things I do that bring about a lot of judgmental looks.

Sometimes, I do Bollywood dancing on my social media platforms. It's my form of expression, and it may not suit some people's perceptions of how a CEO should be.

I have a YouTube channel where I'm frank about my struggles and life experiences. The topics I cover may seem unnatural to some people. I also have my own podcast where I am entirely myself. I laugh about my mistakes and share brutal business lessons I've had to go through. Again, this may seem odd to some people because of the picture-perfect image others perceive entrepreneurs to have.

When this book is published, I will be an author and probably one of the very, very few four-figure entrepreneurs to write a book about their experience so far. I know there will be a few people who may question that or find it weird because I haven't hit their definition of success, but I will continue doing what *I* want to do.

My entire entrepreneurial journey so far is defined by my ideals, my end goals, and my personality. It may not resonate with some people's version of what my journey should be like, and that's okay with me.

As much as I'd like to tell you that no one will judge you, I can't.

When you decide to start your business, you will have a few people whispering behind your back, laughing at how ridiculous your decision sounds to them.

When you decide to start your own YouTube channel, you'll probably have a few people nitpicking how you look in your first video.

When you record your first podcast episode, you'll have a few people talking about it only because they think your voice is too shrill.

The point is, if you're doing something different, you will have people judging you. They judge because they are projecting their own insecurities.

They didn't start a business because they weren't confident in their abilities, so instead, they laugh at you in hopes of diminishing your confidence.

They didn't start a YouTube channel because they feared how their first video would look, so they nitpick yours.

They didn't record their first podcast episode because they didn't think anyone else would like how they sounded. So they judge your voice when you do it.

They do it because if they get to you and you stop doing what you wanted to do, then, in a way, there is justification for the reasons why *they* couldn't go through with it.

It has absolutely nothing to do with you or your capabilities and not even how they feel about you. It's just them and their insecurities.

That's a messy internal struggle, and we should only feel sorry for them. If only they could just take one step to overcome their insecurities, maybe they would be able to view the world in a better light.

But it's not on you to help them fix their insecurities.

Your job is to continue doing what you want to do.

Your job is to keep going despite all the judgmental looks you will get. And oh boy, you're going to get quite a few.

Your job is to realize that you are only responsible for your own insecurities, and that's it.

Here's another way I look at it:

If you don't do something, you will be judged. If you do something, you will be judged. Regardless, you already have an ongoing list of people judging you. What's one more person judging you?

If people are judging you, that's on them. If they refuse to acknowledge the fantastic things you do, that's on them. If they want to make you feel inadequate, that's on them. You do not, and I repeat this, you do not need to shine any less to match the darkness they are comfortable with.

If you want to start your business, start it.

If you want to publish your first blog post, then hit that "Publish" button.

If you want to talk about your products/services, talk about them.

This is **YOUR** life. Don't let someone else's problems and insecurities guide your life. You get to choose what you want to do; I think that's the best part of it all!

While they may be in the wrong, it is on you to control the narrative by keeping your head held high. You don't need to stoop to their level or retaliate.

Keeping your head held high regardless of how people treat you gives you control over the situation and allows you to end the situation in a way that helps you the best.

You'll slowly realize that the more you continue doing what you want, the easier it gets to immerse in the experience and ignore the ones who judge you.

So, if you want to do something, go ahead, do it. If you don't want to, again, it's your choice. No one else needs to have a say in it.

In the grand scheme of all the people looking up to you, what's one more person judging you?

2.6

It helps if you can learn to appreciate and enjoy the process.

I chuckled when I wrote this lesson's title.

Ooof, I learned this particular lesson after a lot of annoyance and stubbornness.

As humans, I think it is in our nature to create timelines for our life. We chalk out the milestones. We think we know when and how things should happen. Degree by twenty-two, married by twenty-five, kids by thirty, promotion to Marketing Manager by thirty-four, CMO by forty, and so on.

Naturally, when I became an entrepreneur, I thought about how things would go. I assumed my own timelines and thought I knew how I would get to where I wanted to be.

It didn't happen that way.

Things were going *so* slow. It just didn't match my timeline at all, and it used to annoy me a lot.

One moment changed how I felt about my journey, and I'd like to share that moment with you.

I consider myself extremely privileged that my parents have always given me a comfortable life. I didn't take money for granted, but at the same time, I will admit that I wasn't fully aware of the value of money. When I started my full-time job, I was a bit more aware as I knew how much time I had to put in to earn money. I was living comfortably with my income.

In all my years, I never had to struggle for money. I had to work for it, yes, but not struggle.

It wasn't until I was a broke entrepreneur that I fully understood the value of money. I was putting in twice-thrice the amount of effort and yet, I was barely making even one-tenth of what I was earning when I had my full-time job.

When you perceive you have money, you manage it from a place of comfort. When you perceive you don't have money, you manage it from a place of fear. That changes the way you handle money. It also changes the actions you take towards money. As I unlearned my money mindset from my full-time job and started to learn a new money mindset as an entrepreneur, I understood how hard it was to make money.

What was previously an expense I wouldn't have given a second thought to, I was now contemplating and debating how much I needed it and whether it was worth the amount I needed to spend. This was out of character for me and one that I didn't know until I spoke to a client a year and a half later.

I was speaking to my client, and by default, I started explaining the value of each resource I recommended to buy for their marketing. I went in-depth and even gave them alternate options if they wanted to use a lower percentage of their budget. My client was impressed that I was sensitive to their budgetary limitations.

At that moment, I appreciated what the process of growing a business as a broke entrepreneur had taught me. I needed to go through that period of being broke. I needed to experience a time where I would break down because I couldn't afford something as simple as \$12. A time when I would feel my anxiety rising while looking at my bank account.

I needed to go through that process to understand what business owners went through. If I was recommending the same products without going through all that I did, I would have assumed that the products were affordable to everyone.

Going through the journey of being broke taught me to have a realistic view of money, and at that moment, I realized that to fully get to where you wish to be, the process is essential. As much as I would have liked to be financially comfortable in the beginning stages of my entrepreneurial journey, I needed to go through it to be a better marketing strategy consultant to my clients.

I stopped doubting the process from that moment on. I no longer questioned why I was going through something and instead began looking for the lessons I had to learn.

While we may hear of people going viral within the first six months of starting their YouTube channel, it is easy to assume that it only took six months to get them to where they are now. What we don't hear is that almost always, there is a journey of time and patience, spanning more than those six months, that got them to where they are.

We hear people becoming millionaires within a year of starting their business, and again, we don't recognize that there is a path that led them to where they are, and that path started even before the year of starting their business.

The universal truth is that it takes time to get to where you want to be. It almost always takes longer than you assume it would.

When we look for the lessons in our journey instead of feeling entitled to success, we start to enjoy the process.

Yes, things are hard and a little rough sometimes, but that only means it is teaching and preparing us for something bigger in the future.

This journey is challenging and always pushes you to be a better version of yourself. But when you look at the journey as a process to prepare you for the end you wish to reach, it makes you feel like there is a purpose to what you are going through. You may or may not understand it in the moment of pain, confusion, and frustration, but learning to trust that the process is teaching you something, changes how you show up. It makes you feel ready to take on any obstacle and helps you keep an open mind as you move through the process.

This may be a bit more on the spiritual side, but I believe that learning to enjoy and appreciate the process is a choice and a choice that we should make every single day.

Regardless of how tough things are, if we each saw our journey as a success in itself, we would feel lucky and privileged that we had the opportunity to pursue something that really lights our souls with passion. That's not something any of us should take for granted.

As much as possible, shouldn't we make it a point to enjoy this beautiful gift we've given ourselves—this journey?

2.7

Your best is going to look different every day.

Let's take a second and analyze our entire lives up until now.

When you were in school, doing your best meant you had to do all your homework, study for your exams, and perform well.

When you were in college, doing your best meant not skipping classes, studying for your tests, and striving to at least pass them.

When you were working, doing your best meant showing up to work on time, completing all the tasks on hand, and going the extra mile.

Never in my life did my playtime or my "relax" time ever make to the list of me doing my best. As I grew older, the perception was that the playtime and break time were just miscellaneous times that would only detract me from working on the things that made me do my best.

I carried the same concept when I started my entrepreneurial journey.

If I was relaxing or watching Netflix, my mind would be racing and wondering why I wasn't "doing my best". After all, I had put so much on the line to become an entrepreneur, so why was I not working twenty-four/seven?

I would feel guilty on the days I took a break. In some odd way, I thought I was letting myself down.

When I was trying to watch a nice K-drama on Netflix, my mind would ask me why I wasn't watching something marketing related on YouTube instead.

My mind just couldn't wrap around the fact that anything less than a ten-hour workday was still me doing my best.

I didn't allow myself to enjoy the time when I was relaxing. When I was working, I wondered when I'd get to relax. It was a vicious cycle.

Over time, I really began to question if this was how I wanted my journey to be.

I asked myself multiple times, and my answer was evident each time. I didn't want to continue this journey if it meant being "on" twenty-four/seven. I started this journey to give myself the freedom to choose, and I had been depriving myself of the freedom I was working so hard to get.

That didn't seem right at all. Instead of controlling every single action of mine, I let loose, and started trusting my gut.

I would take a break if I felt I needed to take a break. No questions asked.

If I felt I wanted to take a whole day off, again, no judgment.

If I wanted to pull an all-nighter, I would do it, and I wouldn't second guess my decision.

If I wanted to work only three hours that day, I would do it happily.

If I felt like cuddling up in my blanket, watching my favorite K-drama, munching on ice cream for a few hours, no questions asked.

In each one of those cases, I was still doing my best. My best didn't fit the standard perception, but it was my version of doing my best, and that was enough for me.

We put so much pressure on ourselves to be our best every day. We don't even realize that there is no particular way to be our best.

We have to learn to be open-minded about what our best could look like. It's on us to change the narrative by removing existing notions about what we think our best should look like. Instead, we should learn to recognize and accept all the versions of us doing our best.

Somedays, your best will look like a ten-hour workday.

Somedays, your best will be you out on holiday with your family.

Other days, it's creating content for a few hours.

Other times, it's doing a puzzle or painting your nails.

So, tell me, what does your best look like today?

CHAPTER 3
BUSINESS STRATEGY

Dream ✓

Strategize ✓

Take Action ✓

One step at a time.

3.1

There are only three steps to become a digital entrepreneur.

Before starting this journey, I never understood the exact process behind creating something on my own.

Sure, you see the businesses selling their products, but what happens on the backend? How does it all come together? Where do you start?

As a marketer, I knew it starts from an idea, but how did one go from conceptualizing that to a full-blown business?

The thing about this entrepreneurial journey is that you don't know it until you get into it. You learn as you go. You learn one step, and then the next step becomes evident. And then you learn the new step, and so on.

When I look back at how I started, I see many steps I took to start my online business. But if I must take a bird's eye view of the entire process, I believe there were only three main steps. If you're looking to get started, then these three steps should be what you focus on:

Step 1: Find a platform to sell on.

When I knew I wanted to create a digital product that would help people with their LinkedIn profiles, the first thing I did was research for various platforms I could sell it on.

I made a list of my requirements to sell a digital product online. I then looked at the pros and cons of each available platform.

I didn't have a huge following then, so I expected only a few people to buy the product. If I were opting for a platform, I wanted to ensure the product paid for itself. I couldn't afford the extra money to pay for the platform, especially when I wasn't sure how many sales the product could make each month.

I chose my website as the platform for my first few products. I was already paying the monthly fees so having a digital product on the website didn't change how much I was spending each month.

For my seventh product, a membership program to help business owners and entrepreneurs with their marketing, I decided to change my website platform to another one that was priced higher. I moved forward with the new website platform because it could support the membership program. By then, my income was much steadier, and my business had reached a point where my website needed to look highly professional.

The new platform offered better features and gave my business a premium look. It had its own extensive automation for marketing too. All in all, I loved it, and I went ahead with it. The membership program was a super niched product, charged at a premium price, and the new website platform was a good fit. The membership program actually paid for the new website platform each month.

My point is that choosing the right platform for your digital product is essential. If you don't have a huge following, you might want to consider selling your digital product on a platform that offers its own users. That way, you don't feel pressured to bring in your own traffic every month. This was one of the reasons why I started my Etsy digital shop and became a teacher on Skillshare.

A platform enabling you to drive traffic will be a better option if you have a considerable following or a higher-priced niched product.

I can't definitively tell you which one is the best.

Here are a few questions that can help you decide:

- ♦ What kind of product am I selling? Does the platform have systems and additional features to support the product?

- ♦ Who am I selling it to? Do I want to tap into the platform's users, or do I bring in the customers for my product?

- ♦ Does the platform fit within my current resources?

Step 2: Figure out how your customer gets the product and how you will get paid.

If you are using third-party platforms with their existing users, then this step is usually taken care of by those platforms. You may need to add your details and run around a bit to make sure your payment account is verified, but for the most part, this step is not too problematic in this case.

You need to give this step more thought if you are handling the process yourself.

My sixth product was a five-day email course for Instagram, and again, I had maxed out the number of products on my website. For this product, I added a form on my sales page, and when people signed up for the course, I sent them an automated email with the details to pay for the course using the third-party payment platform. Once the payment was made, I would manually begin their email automation. I wasn't expecting too many people to sign up for this course because of my low following, so making the process semi-manual made sense for me at the time.

Again, as my business grew, I couldn't invest the time to do this manually, so I shifted to a website platform that covered everything I needed for my digital products and marketing consultancy firm. The new website platform

I chose also had the features to handle payment and email automation for my clients, so this step was taken care of.

This step is crucial because as a digital entrepreneur, your entire business is online.

The smoother this step is for your customers, the more value it adds to your online business. Especially when you are starting out, it helps to keep this step as simple as possible.

Here are a few questions to help you out:

♦ Can they find my product sales page with ease?

♦ Can they buy my product with ease?

♦ How will I get paid?

♦ Is there a smooth integration between the platform and the third-party payment app?

Step 3: Create paths for people to find your product.

This, of course, is the marketing aspect of your business. Even if you are on a platform with users to buy your product, you need to create more paths for people to find your product.

Even though my products are on Etsy, and I get a steady flow of sales because of the SEO on Etsy, I still talk about my products on my Instagram page. I add the links to the Etsy products in the description of my YouTube videos and my Podcast description links.

As of March 2022, even with a small following like mine, these social media platforms contribute to at least 20% of my Etsy traffic each month, which is pretty awesome.

This step is probably the most significant in the entire process. It is also the step that takes the longest to implement.

Here are a few questions that can help you out:

♦ Where can I connect with my potential customers?

♦ How do I lead my potential customers to my product?

You may have an excellent product. A product that makes a difference to the people around you and contributes to your business revenue.

But if people aren't finding it, then people aren't buying it. That's just the rules of the game. We'll go in depth about creating paths in the Marketing chapter [Section 4.2].

It doesn't have to be complicated to start something on your own as a digital entrepreneur. If you get these three steps right, you have a firm foundation to build your business.

Firm foundation, strong building, right?

If you visit <u>www.themarketingnomad.co/zero-to-four-figures</u>, you'll get access to a printable workbook to implement this framework.

3.2

There is something called "too much planning".

In December 2019, the bidding war on freelance platforms started getting to me.

After a point, I succumbed to the pressure and started bidding on the low end. Since my bid was low, the money coming was not enough to sustain my journey.

I knew that if I wanted to bring my business to a place where I was earning my time's worth, I had to start creating new income streams. I was frustrated about not being compensated adequately for my time, so I began looking for more passive options. I wanted to break free from the "time equals money" equation.

Around this time, a friend of mine from high school reached out to me via LinkedIn and asked if I could review their LinkedIn profile. They were applying for jobs, and they wanted my opinion.

While I had attended a few workshops on how to craft the perfect LinkedIn profile in 2018 and reviewed the LinkedIn profiles of my friends when I was in my MBA program, I had never charged for it before.

When my friend said they would be happy to compensate for my time, I accepted the project.

After I was done, my entrepreneurial mind started racing. What if I created a course that taught people how to craft their LinkedIn profiles independently? It didn't involve much on my end except developing and marketing the course. The course fit my whole agenda of creating a passive income stream.

I was excited about the idea because I knew my product could help people.

I sat on this idea for eight weeks.

Eight. Weeks. Two Whole Months.

I kept justifying that I needed my product to be perfect. The course material, the designs, the branding, the flow of the course, and all that jazz.

I claimed I was in "planning" mode, but in reality, I was just too chicken to take the next step.

I was procrastinating, and I didn't realize it. It was the first time I was creating and launching a product. All eyes were going to be on me. It was one thing to be applying for jobs on freelance platforms where all the rejections were private. For this product, I needed to show up on my social media pages and talk about it.

I wasn't ready for that. Instead of acknowledging that I wasn't prepared, I kept delaying by saying the product wasn't "structured" yet.

It wasn't until mid-February 2020 that I gave myself a hard deadline—I had to launch my product in two weeks or drop the idea altogether.

Giving myself an ultimatum helped me put my plan into immediate action. Instead of nitpicking at every single move, I opened Canva and started to create the workbook.

I also learned how to set up a digital shop on my website. I planned a ten-day launch. I created content about my product and how it would make a difference in the lives of job hunters.

That was the first and the last time I ever took my sweet time to "plan". Now, whenever I need to plan, I set a deadline for when I want to wrap up the new project.

As a business owner and/or an entrepreneur, most of the projects you take up will be new ventures for your business. This means that you're almost always going to be in unknown territory. This can make you feel vulnerable sometimes, and there is always a higher likelihood of you continuing to "plan" as a cover for procrastination.

The next time you want to plan something, know that it's a good thing to plan. But you have to recognize the point when planning becomes procrastination because there is something called "too much planning".

Some of the signs of procrastination would be:

- ◆ When you keep putting off doing something because you want to "feel ready for it".

- ◆ Each time you use the phrase "This has to be perfect" in your planning process

- ◆ When you find yourself nitpicking every detail of your plan

- ◆ When you really want to do something but you "haven't found the time" or "there have been other things on your plate" and suddenly it's been weeks since you last worked on it

If you find yourself constantly in the planning phase but never in the implementation phase, then giving yourself a hard deadline is one of the simplest ways to help you get going. Your mind draws comfort from the fact that you will always be around to do the task.

When you give yourself a hard deadline, you're telling your mind that you will walk away when the time comes. If the task means something to you, you will move heaven and earth to finish it before the deadline. If the deadline passes and you haven't done anything about it, you'll know the task wasn't your priority, and you won't waste further time thinking about it. You can move on to the next task on hand.

Either way, that's a win for you, right?

3.3

The advice and tips you get should only be a starting point.

As I hopped on this journey, I found advice and tips on every corner.

There were people in the digital entrepreneurial field who I looked up to, and I thought that if I hung on to every word they said, I would get to where they were. But I quickly learned that I couldn't implement most of the advice and tips I got. Not just that, even the ones that I could apply, I needed to tweak them to match my business.

It wasn't that the advice from other digital entrepreneurs wasn't good. It was that their advice was coming from *their* place of experience. Their experience was not always the go-to advice for my business because the factors affecting it were different.

I'll give you an example. In June 2020, I enrolled in a course to help me advance in the consultation field. The course aimed to help one find clients on social media platforms.

I soon realized that the course was more helpful for people with at least 10,000 followers on their social media platforms. Not just that, the course was meant for people who could afford a significant investment in ads and buy expensive software for the launch. "Expensive" in my perception, given my zero-bank balance, but to someone else with at least six figures in their bank account, these suggestions may have been cost-effective and worthwhile expenses.

I wasn't there yet. I couldn't afford the $300 client relationship management platform that this course recommended. I couldn't afford to outsource the "non-CEO" tasks, nor could I spend four or five figures on ads. I had less than 500 followers then and expecting even ten of them to show up for my launch was a huge stretch.

Most of the advice in the course was not meant for someone like me, though there were some pieces of advice that I tweaked to match my capabilities.

For example, instead of opting for the $300 client relationship management platform *(mainly because it was $300 out of my price range)*, I took the *concept* of the processes and applied it to my business.

I replicated the systems of the client management platform using my existing resources. I created a process so my client would fill out a form I made from my email marketing platform. Then, I automated email instructions for them to pay via a third-party payment platform. I manually created each invoice and sent it to my clients. I also had set up an automation where my client would receive a prompt to leave me a review after 90 days of working with me.

To create this process, I didn't invest more than I already had. I couldn't implement the advice and the tips directly, but it gave me a starting point for my business.

Each time I give advice to anyone on any of my social media platforms, I always say:

"My advice and tips should only be a starting point for creating processes that work specifically for you and your business."

That includes this book that you're reading right now. My advice in this book should only be a starting point for you. You have to see what applies to you and what doesn't.

When you look at other digital entrepreneurs, including me, you must understand that our advice comes from the journey we've had. We've had different experiences because of our strengths, weaknesses, existing resources, finances, mindset, limitations, and other factors like our city, family support, race, religion, etc. Our advice comes from all the factors that make up our journey. Those factors may or may not apply to your journey.

Take me, for example. I'm an Indian. I'm a woman. I'm a millennial.

These are factored into the decisions I make for my business. Another fact about me is that I put in all my savings to start this business and let's face it, that wasn't much considering I had only worked full-time for a year. I did not take financial support from anyone. So yes, I started this journey broke. That was a factor that contributed to almost every decision in my business.

But on the other hand, I would consider myself privileged that I'm living with my parents as of 2022, and I don't have to worry about paying rent, paying off my car, or even paying car insurance. *(Thanks, mom and dad!)* Again, that factors into the decisions I make for my business.

My journey will be vastly different from someone who has to pay off their student loan or has significant financial backing. Each person's journey is unique.

That's just how it is.

The advice from other digital entrepreneurs may or may not align with where you are. Maybe I would have easily implemented the advice from the course if my business was at a different stage, but from where I was, I couldn't.

Any time you receive advice or tips, take a second to see if it actually works for you and your business, given the growth stage.

You can ask yourself the following questions:

- ◆ Does this tip apply to my business? *(Consider various factors like your industry, target audience, competitors, environment, etc.)*

- Does this tip work to my advantage?

- Does this tip make use of my strengths and existing resources?

- If I implement this tip, will it leave me in a better or worse place?

- If this tip is not a good fit for me, how can I tweak it to fit my business' needs?

It's not that the advice you get doesn't work. It's that sometimes, the advice you get may not be compatible with the factors that contribute to you/your business. So, graciously accept any advice you get but also know that it should only be a starting point for you.

Over time of asking yourself these questions before you implement any advice/tip, you'll be able to tune better into your instincts and create systems that work just for you. Isn't that awesome?

3.4

Plan backward.

After seeing my envisioned future come crashing down in June 2019, I felt there was no point in planning for the future.

So, when I started my entrepreneurial journey in September 2019, I refused to acknowledge where I wanted to be a year from then because all I had previously dreamed of was gone.

In my spite, I refused to plan for my entrepreneurial journey when I started. I didn't know what was going to happen in a year. I did not *want* to know. I was adamant not to even think about it. I just knew that if I didn't make enough money to survive by the following year, I would quit and apply for a full-time job.

What was the point of planning if it wasn't going to happen?

Why did I even need to see where I could be a year from now if it was just going to be taken away from me?

These were the thoughts swimming in my mind for a very long time.

In hindsight, I think I just didn't have it in me to hope again. I couldn't bear to put myself through the pain of wishing for something and have it all crash.

So, I only focused on taking the next step.

Buying a domain for myself.

Creating a website.

Getting out of bed before 10 a.m. every day.

Having breakfast.

Cooking at least one meal a day.

Listing out my skills.

Putting my profile up on freelance websites.

Applying for at least three projects every day.

Work on my first project.

Continue applying for new projects.

Work on the next project.

And so on and so forth.

To be honest, as I'm writing this book, I don't remember feeling anything during the first few months of my entrepreneurial journey. I was doing the task on hand, the next, and then the next. I was taking things day by day, week by week, and going with the flow.

Around February 2020, I started gaining recognition on freelance platforms. I had a few potential clients reaching out to me. People wanted to work with me. People started acknowledging that my knowledge and skills could help them with their business. People liked how dedicated I was.

Each of these moments of recognition healed parts of me, little by little.

By the end of February 2020, I had a few clients, and because of the small successes I was having, somewhere in the corner of my heart, I knew I could go somewhere on this journey.

As I started to feel this, the question arose, *"Where?"*

Where could I take this? What exactly did a "Successful Entrepreneur" even mean to me?

I had taken inspiration from Sara Blakely, but that was *her* journey. Where did *I* want to take this?

It was clear that I wasn't going to quit after the first year, so how long would I keep going on this journey?

As scared as I was to hope, I knew that I would continue feeling lost if I didn't have a definite vision for the future. Without a plan, I wouldn't be able to recognize where I wanted to head to.

I gingerly opened my business journal.

I looked at the page where I had previously mapped out the kind of person I had to be. As I looked through each point I had written, I knew I was getting there slowly.

A small smile slipped.

I took a fresh sheet, took a deep breath, and wrote these words in the middle of the page:

"Where do I see myself in one year?"

I drew a cloud around it because we now know I stared at those words a little too long, and I didn't want to feel awkward about it.

And then I started writing. I started with the simple things—where I wished to see my social media accounts after one year or the products I wanted to launch by the one-year mark.

Then I moved to the bigger things.

My business revenue at the one-year mark.

My business *impact* at the one-year mark.

My impact at the one-year mark.

My *legacy* at the one-year mark.

After filling the entire page, I felt like my old self again. Mapping out one year added something concrete to my plans. I wasn't in the air anymore; I was grounded. I had an endpoint for the year.

Wait a minute. I had an endpoint. Not the route.

I didn't know *how* I was going to get to the endpoint. Was that what was missing all those years of me mapping my life out, I wondered.

I looked back.

I had magnificent five, ten, and even twenty-year goals before, but I never thought about **how** I would achieve them. I just thought I'd figure it out somewhere along the way, and frankly, I never achieved any of those goals.

I always blamed it on external circumstances; now, it was clear that that was my own doing.

I had goals, yes, but those goals were too far off for me to see if I was on the right track towards them. For example, five years was a long time, and as the days went by, I never bothered to see if I was heading toward my goals or not.

I didn't have smaller goals to let me know if I was going in the right direction.

So, I looked down at my sheet of paper.

One year. Twelve months.

That's a long time of me continuously working without knowing if I was in alignment with my goals or not. I broke down my goals into quarters. On the next page, I started setting my targets for each quarter to get to my final one-year target. For example, if I wanted 1000 followers by the end of the one-year mark, and I assumed a 10% growth quarter on quarter, then that meant I should be aiming for 215 followers in the first quarter, 237 followers in the second quarter, then 261 in the third, and lastly, 287 in the last quarter.

Yes, I agree; I'm a total math nerd. But don't worry:

Visit www.themarketingnomad.co/zero-to-four-figures to access an excel sheet that will help you calculate your numbers for quarters, months, and weeks according to the growth rate you wish to achieve. Now you don't have to do the math *wink*

Back to my story. I did the same with other tangible and intangible aspects of my business. Now that I had broken down each of those goals into monthly and weekly goals, it was easier for me to write actionable steps. If I wanted to hit a growth of x followers on Instagram for this month, I had to post a total of y amount of content or $y/4$ amount of content for the week.

I set up an excel sheet and started tracking. I picked the first Sunday of every month to look at the stats for the previous month.

My first draft wasn't the most accurate. Some targets were unreasonable, but it didn't matter. I just readjusted them along the way.

As the weeks passed and I evaluated my progress, I felt like I was flowing. There were some months I hit my targets and some months I didn't. But either way, I knew the direction I was heading. I could see the path to my one-year goal, which changed the game for me.

Having a goal wasn't a reminder of what I wasn't achieving. It became a reminder of what I should be putting my efforts into. It gave me a starting point for the steps I needed to take to reach those targets.

Everything in my business started aligning with my plan, including me setting up my company, hitting the revenue goals steadily, increasing my passive income streams, and so on.

When 2020 ended, I felt very confident about the one-year plan I had made. That plan gave me direction, and I knew planning backward was working for me. I even set out to create a five-year plan for my business.

Ambitious, I know, but that was probably the best step I took for my business.

As a matter of fact, writing this book was a part of the plan, and my book launch was planned for Year 2, which was 2022. I worked backward to figure out when to start the outline for the book, write the book, hire an editor, and so on. Given this book was my first book, I was flexible on the timeline. There were a few delays but planning backward helped me stay on track to hit my goal.

Here's how you can plan backward for yourself:

Step 1: Set a timeframe. *(Six months, one year, five years, etc.)*

Step 2: Write down what you wish to accomplish by the end of that timeframe.

Step 3: Divide the timeframe into years (if applicable), quarters, then months, then weeks, then days.

Step 4: As you divide the timeframe, break down the goal into smaller goals.

Step 5: Write actionable steps to accomplish each of the smaller goals.

If you did a one-year plan, it should look something like this:

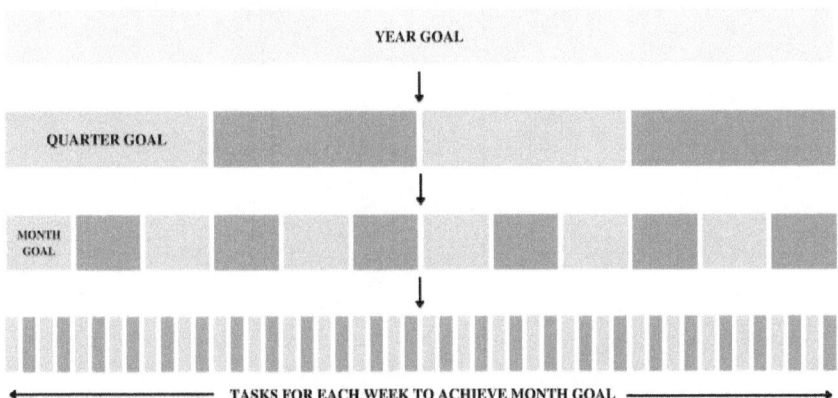

Having goals is great but working backward is the magic process to help you achieve them in your chosen timeline.

Isn't my book in your hands proof that this method works?

Visit www.themarketingnomad.co/zero-to-four-figures to get access to a printable workbook that will help you plan backward.

3.5

The "If... then" Strategy.

The story starts during my college days.

Whenever my friends and I wanted to skip class, I'd think of various possibilities and prepare ourselves for it.

If we got caught... then what would we say?

We all had to come up with the same story, right?

If someone's parent caught us on the street somewhere *(and this did happen)* ... then what would be our plan?

I had thought of every single situation and how to handle it. As a classic overthinker, I had taken it upon myself to be the one to find every possible outcome and our respective reactions to it.

It gave me some semblance of control and helped me be more present as I bunked classes with my friends.

That was a strategy I called the *"If... then"* strategy.

When I started this entrepreneurial journey, I was recovering from the constant anxious thoughts that surfaced as an aftermath of the visa situation.

Meditation was helping a lot, and as time went by, my anxious thoughts were slowly reducing, but there were these sporadic anxiety attacks that I was still unable to overcome.

I would be completely normal one minute, writing something in my business journal, and I'd suddenly feel my heart rate increase. With no warning, I'd have a swarm of anxious thoughts.

Was I going to make it? Would I manage to earn a consistent income? Would I be able to live up to what people expected? Was this product going to make any sales? What if I never get another client?

This happened a few times before I remembered what I used to do in the high-pressure bunking situations during my college days and how I managed to enjoy being in the present—my "If... then" strategy!

It always gave me control over my thoughts back in the day, and I wondered if I could apply it to my business.

So, I opened my personal journal and started writing every anxious thought that came into my mind.

I thought about what could happen next and how I would deal with it.

For example:

If this entrepreneurial journey did not work out for me... *then* I would just put my resume on LinkedIn, apply to full-time jobs, and move forward from there."

If this product didn't do well... *then* I would analyze what was lacking and create another one within a month.

If I couldn't earn a consistent income... *then* I would steadily increase my passive income streams.

One by one, each of my anxious questions was getting answered.

This method worked, and I started to feel more in control of my thoughts. I got comfortable with the possible outcomes of any step I took. I was optimistic, but at the same time, I was ready to handle whatever else came my way. I started feeling more present and enjoying every aspect of my day-to-day activities for my business.

Now it's true that I couldn't think of every possible outcome, but this entire process made me feel more confident in my abilities. If I had a plan to handle the adverse outcomes I had thought of, I could handle any other possible adverse outcomes.

I've found that the "If... then" strategy works well because it not only encourages you to be more present but also doesn't assume that everything will go perfectly. It mentally prepares you for the worst-case scenarios.

Here's how you can do the "If... then" strategy for yourself:

Step 1: Take a piece of paper and a pen.

Step 2: Draw a line in the center, dividing the entire page half.

Step 3: Label the left column as "If" and the right column as "Then".

Step 4: Write all the possible outcomes on the left side. It helps to get all your thoughts out before moving on to the right side.

Step 5: For each possible outcome in the "If" column, write your thoughts on how you would handle it.

Your page should look something like this:

IF	THEN
I don't hit four figures next month	*I will reach out to old clients to request for referrals.*
I don't get any new followers this month	*I will send voice notes to existing followers and ask them how my content can be more relevant to them.*
The new income stream does not have a good return-on-investment.	*I go back to the drawing board and evaluate if I want to continue or scrap it.*

Note: I'm not saying that this is how to deal with anxiety, as each person's coping mechanisms are different. This method worked for me personally. Of course, I always advocate seeking help if you feel you need it.

Especially at the beginning of this journey, you'll be disappointed a lot. Not because you're doing something wrong, but because of the natural tendency to have unrealistic expectations in the beginning. You're new to the scene; there's a lot of excitement. After hearing all those success stories around you, you feel everything will click right away.

It doesn't happen that way at all.

You quickly realize that the route to success is long, oh *so* long, and filled with many, many disappointments. I don't mean to be a bummer, but this is the journey's reality.

The good news is that you learn how to be more realistic with your expectations over time.

Not to say that disappointments cease to exist as time goes by, but the gap between your expectation and reality reduces, which helps you cope with the disappointments better.

Having the "If... then" Strategy in place keeps you grounded. It also helps you to cope with disappointments.

When you plan multiple routes for yourself, you start adjusting your expectations to match the spectrum of best to worst-case scenarios.

Yes, of course, sometimes negative outcomes will happen.

My first three product launches did not make a single sale. Because of my "If... then" Strategy, I knew I had to analyze what went wrong and release a better product within a month.

I remember being sad during my first product launch. It was because of unhealthy expectations. The weight of my expectations was so much that I stopped promoting after three days.

I had a more realistic expectation for the subsequent two launches, and even though I didn't make any sales, I wasn't disappointed. I had hoped for at least one or two sales, and when that didn't happen, I took it as a new starting point and kept putting my foot forward.

I continued to analyze what went wrong and fixed those problems for the following product I launched.

I had less than five sales in total until my sixth product launch, and finally, forty people in my seventh product launch. All this was when I was with less than 1,000 followers on Instagram.

The same went for my Etsy shop. I made six sales in January 2021 with the first product I launched. I had hoped for ten.

According to my "If... then" Strategy, I had to keep adding more products to the mix if I didn't hit my target sales. And that's what I did. I kept going.

And what do ya know, I made forty-five sales in January 2022, with seven unique products in my listings.

When things don't go as you hoped, you stop looking at them as "worst case scenarios" but instead as one of the possible routes the journey could take you on. It becomes easier to think of these outcomes as routes that give you a new start point rather a failure point.

All I want to say is that it's okay to hope for the best. It's healthy even to hope for the best. But doesn't preparing for other possible outcomes help you stay ahead?

If you visit www.themarketingnomad.co/zero-to-four-figures, you'll get access to a printable workbook to help you implement the "If... then" Strategy.

3.6

You are your most important case study.

Reading and analyzing case studies was my favorite part of my MBA days.

I loved reading about the unique situations that businesses were in and how they tackled those challenges. I would sit in the library with my cup of hot chocolate and read those pages intently. I'd highlight the critical parts, write down short notes on the side, and relate the case studies to concepts I had read in class. I had this secret wish that someday, my company would be the one they wrote about in a case study. I had no clue what my company would be but thinking about that always brought a smile.

When I started my business, I applied the same analysis to every aspect of my business. Every scenario in my business was documented in my business journal. That included documenting my thoughts while those situations played out and writing down how I navigated my business through those situations.

I did this because I knew the factors that affected my business were unique. As much as I learned from other business case studies, I knew that analyzing my business would help me the most in the future. In fact, I don't think I would have been able to write this book if I didn't have a business journal.

While case studies can help you understand how other businesses have navigated through their situations, those solutions may or may not apply to your business. Their results culminate in the unique factors that affected the business in question, which may or may not be the same factors that affect your business.

When you analyze your current standing and how that relates to each situation your business faces, it puts you in a pivotal position to study strategies that work specifically for your business.

There is no cookie-cutter solution to deal with situations your business finds itself in. Knowing what to tweak according to your business needs is essential. It is difficult to understand how to apply a solution to your business if you haven't taken the time to analyze your business.

I have a business journal where I write everything that goes on in my business. It isn't fancy. It's just a five-subject plain notebook, and I keep writing daily.

Here's what goes into my business journal:

- Situations or problems I'm currently dealing with

- My thoughts about why I made a particular decision.

- End results of the decision

- Thoughts about the end results and see if there was any way I could improve the outcome for the next time.

- Some tips and tricks I've picked up along the way.

This business journal has helped me in unimaginable ways. There have been times when I have gotten additional information to make better decisions by just looking at my past choices. I highly recommend keeping a business journal for your business.

Here's how you can get started on your business journal:

Step 1: Get a notebook *(preferably one with many pages).*

Step 2: Every time you write in your book, start with the day and date. If needed, add in the time as well.

Step 3: Write down the current situation or problem you are facing. Explain in detail. The more information you can add, the easier it will be for you to reference in the future.

Step 4: Write down your thoughts on the situation or problem. If you have a few solutions in your mind, write them out. You can list each solution's pros and cons and possible outcomes you could expect from it.

Step 5: Continue adding new situations, problems, or decisions in the book as you go.

Step 6: If you've taken a decision or an action to solve the problem, write down *why* you chose that decision. This is very important.

Step 7: Once some time has passed, write your observations about the consequences of your decision. Was it a positive or negative outcome? What else contributed to the success/failure of that decision? Would you have done anything differently?

Step 8: Keep looking back and reading what you've written previously. It helps to remind yourself every now and then about the situations and decisions you've made so far. If there's an old decision that influences your current decision, make a note of it.

Also, you don't have to leave space. If you have more thoughts to add later on, write them on a new page with the date. You can always add a note (or a post-it) to remind yourself that you've continued on another page.

The more you document everything, the more data you will have when making future decisions. Data is power when it comes to growing your business, and over time, that data will help you recognize unique factors that influence your business.

A successful entrepreneur isn't someone who knows what to do. A successful entrepreneur is someone who knows what to do *by considering their business's unique factors and working it to their advantage.*

Those few extra words make a world of difference, don't they?

3.7

Segregate your week by your activities.

As a digital entrepreneur with her own YouTube channel, podcast, Etsy shop, Instagram page, and consulting clients, it's needless to say that planning my time is essential to my success in balancing my various roles.

I used to plan my week the same way everyone else usually does. I would get my planner out, open it to two blank pages side by side, and then draw six vertical lines, with the third line overlapping the book's center. I'd also draw a horizontal line at the top of the pages to write the day and date in the boxes. I'd then proceed to write down my tasks for each day.

While this helped me manage my time to a moderate extent, my weekly planner was also confusing for me because there were so many things I was supposed to focus on. I needed a clearer planner, so I kept experimenting with different ways of planning my day.

Over time, I created a method that worked for me.

For those of you who juggle multiple roles, I believe my new technique of planning one's week will help you manage your time better. I hope you can use this technique as a starting point to create a planner that works for you.

The Activity Segregated Weekly (ASW) Planner:

Step 1: Either take a blank sheet of paper in landscape or a book and open it to two consecutive blank pages.

Step 2: Draw six vertical lines with the third line overlapping the center of the book (if you're doing this in a book)

Step 3: Draw six horizontal lines over the rest of the page. You should have six rows. I'll explain what each row is for, and based on that, you can determine how much space you'd like to leave for each row.

Here's a picture of what your page(s) should look like:

Now let me explain what each row is for:

Row 1: Day and Date

This is where you will write the day and date.

Row 2: Repetitive Tasks

Now for me, I have repetitive tasks that I do every single day. These include journaling, doing yoga, or posting content on my Instagram stories to engage with my followers.

These are critical tasks to my business's overall well-being and growth, and I cannot skip these. I add self-care tasks like meditation, journaling, and yoga/exercise because those are integral to how I show up for my business. I've talked about adding self-care activities into the work calendar in the Growth Mindset chapter [Section 5.4], so I'm not going to elaborate here.

Row 3: Your Tasks for the Day

These are the usual tasks you would have for each day. They could include things like submitting a proposal for your potential client, or in my case, recording a YouTube video or a podcast episode, etc.

Row 4: Tracker

In my business, there are some stats that I need to track. For example, when writing this book, I added the word count in the tracker section of my planner. This was to help me check my progress and ensure I was pacing myself correctly. You can add whatever you like in this section. For example, you can track your anxiety/stress level, cold emails/calls, your work breaks, etc.

Row 5: Reminders

For me, this section has my content uploads and my submissions. I have a few content pieces that are weekly and monthly. This section helps me stick to my schedule and reminds me to announce the release of the content pieces.

For example, sometimes, I will create and schedule a content piece a few days or weeks in advance. When the content is released, this section reminds me to talk about it on my Instagram stories or share the content on my other social media pages.

I also add in my submissions in this section. For example, if I have to submit a proposal to a client by a specific date, I add it to the date it needs to be submitted.

You can use this section to remind yourself of anything you'd like.

Row 6: Appointments

This section is for all your appointments. I like to mention the time and who I have a meeting with.

Here's a representation of what each row is for *(I usually remember it by keeping one word/short form for each row, and I've added that in brackets)*:

Row 1: Day and Date
Row 2: Repetitive Tasks [REPEAT]
Row 3: Your Tasks for the Day [TASKS]
Row 4: Tracker [TRACK]
Row 5: Reminders [REMIND]
Row 6: Appointments [APPT]

Here's a representation of what my weekly planner looks like:

Day Date	Mon 4/18	Tues 4/19	Wed 4/20	Thurs 4/21	Fri 4/22	Sat 4/23	Sun 4/24
REPEAT	▫ Journal ▫Exercise ▫IG Stories	▫ Journal ▫Exercise ▫IG Stories	▫ Journal ▫ Exercise ▫IG Stories	▫ Journal ▫ Exercise ▫IG Stories	▫ Journal ▫ Exercise ▫IG Stories	▫ Journal ▫ Exercise ▫IG Stories	▫ Journal ▫ Exercise ▫IG Stories
TASKS	▫ Shoot a YouTube video ▫Edit YouTube video	▫Draft proposal ▫Fix course details on website	▫Create Etsy product thumbnail ▫Upload product	▫ Record 2 podcast episodes ▫Schedule episodes for next week	▫ Edit blog posts ▫Edit website to match new branding	▫Create new lead magnet ▫Research about latest trends	▫ Plan for next week
TRACK	Book - 60,468 Stress - 8/10	Book - 61,578 Stress - 5/10	Book - 63,988 Stress - 7/10	Book - 64,892 Stress - 4/10	Book - 67,003, Stress - 3/10	Book - 68,348 Stress - 1/10	Book - 70,908 Stress - 2/10
REMIND	▫ IG Post	▫ IG Post ▫ Podcast Episode 65 live	▫30s video	▫ IG Post ▫ LIVE – 9 p.m.	▫ IG Post ▫ Podcast Episode 66 live	▫YouTube video live	
APPT			▫ 10 p.m. - Meeting with xyz		▫ 9 p.m. - Interview with pqr		

With one glance, I can understand what each week looks like for me.

If I'm looking for weekly appointments, my eyes immediately dart to the last row. If I'm looking specifically for information about my book status, again, my eyes know where to look. I'm not scanning the whole page to find the necessary information.

Everything is neatly segregated according to my needs. It may not seem a lot when you hear me say that I'm saving a few seconds of confusion each time I view my planner. But for a digital entrepreneur like me, every second I can save is a second more I can dedicate to bringing in more revenue for my business.

I love this way of planning my week because each of my activities has a place in the planner. Each time I look at the planner, there is a flow to each day I have planned, and I subconsciously apply the same easy flow to my actual day.

You can customize this to your needs and your business. Isn't it easier to tackle your week when you have a strategy?

Visit www.themarketingnomad.co/zero-to-four-figures to get access to a printable workbook to plan your week using this method.

3.8

In today's day and age, it helps to be multi-passionate.

There was a time when people looked down upon picking a career based on passion.

People would always remind me that my career wasn't supposed to be "fun". No one enjoys their job; they would tell me and look at me in amusement. A job was just something one had to mindlessly do so that they could earn money and, well, survive. The money would allow you to enjoy life, but they said the job itself was not meant for you to enjoy.

I hated it when people would tell me that.

The life we're given is so precious. Why would I want to waste forty years of it doing something I was forced to do? Why couldn't I have it both ways? Why couldn't I have a job that I was excited about *and* have the money to enjoy my life?

Again, people would shake their heads. Life doesn't work that way; they would tell me. If you chose a career that you enjoyed, then it was guaranteed that no money would come from it. According to them, no one made good money from having a career in dancing, singing, or doing something they loved. When I pointed out famous dancers and musicians, people would always say they were the exception, not the rule.

As keen as I was to debate with people much older than me, I knew it was a lost cause to keep putting my point of view across.

They weren't ready to see it because, at that time, it wasn't common for people to follow their passion. Even if they did, people were sure that they would fail. You see, in certain societies, at the time, the perception existed that unless you were an Engineer or a Doctor or a Lawyer, you wouldn't achieve success. If you did manage to fight all odds to find success in a field you loved, people wouldn't look at you with the same respect as they would an engineer, doctor, or lawyer. You're supposed to grow to love the field you are forced to choose. You don't choose a field you love.

At the time, it was really frustrating to hear this. Today, I understand why that perception existed. It was hard for people to make it on their own because the resources available were much less. It was also more expensive to pursue something on your own. It makes sense why people thought finding success in pursuing one's passion was the exception, not the rule.

Today, it's a different game. There are so many digital platforms available to help you gain visibility. There are various avenues to monetize, and you can choose the avenues that align with your budget. It's easier now to pursue your passion than a few years ago.

When I started my entrepreneurial journey, again, I felt restricted.

I was passionate about teaching. I was passionate about speaking on topics that mattered to people. I was passionate about sharing my knowledge, be it technical marketing knowledge or even my knowledge about life. I was passionate about Bollywood dancing.

There were so many things that I was passionate about, and everyone around me said I had to just pick one. Some of them had succeeded in their field, while some were keen observers of the latest trends.

For the first year and a half of my journey, I felt pressure to pick just one thing I was passionate about. I decided on marketing and focused all my efforts on it.

While I loved marketing and happily pursued it as my sole passion, I felt I wasn't using my full potential. There were so many things I was passionate about, and why did I have to suppress them? Why couldn't I find ways to incorporate them into my career?

I felt myself in a familiar situation when I expressed my thoughts again. That's really not how this works, people would say. I heard more people ask, *"Shouldn't you feel lucky that you at least get to pursue one passion?"*

Some of those people even prophesied a definite doom for my career if I added more things to the mix.

It wasn't that I was being ungrateful. It was just that I wanted to do as much as I could do instead of narrowing my focus to one thing. I didn't understand why following your passion meant following only *one* passion.

Here's what I came to realize.

People didn't know what would happen if someone were to show up as a multi-passionate person. There was a norm and a concrete path that previous entrepreneurs had taken to find their success.

That path was to have one passion and one passion alone. In people's minds, it was a path that had proven successful, and to them, a proven approach to success was always the only way to go. Like my engineering days, anything that wasn't proven before was looked down upon.

I focused only on one passion for one and a half years. I would watch other digital entrepreneurs follow their passion. Some of these passions were things that I, too, was passionate about, but couldn't do, because I had to focus on my love for marketing.

That started to get a little irritating. That irritation got a little bit bigger each time I saw someone else making a YouTube video on a topic that I would have loved to make but couldn't because it wasn't about marketing.

This feeling grew until I could no longer take it.

I didn't succumb to people's expectations when I was twenty years old, and I wasn't going to start now.

I changed the content on my social media platforms to align it with my other passions. I kept my podcast for my marketing, business, and mindset tips. I started making YouTube videos on my life experiences and the lessons I had learned so far. I created a course on Limiting Beliefs on a learning platform. I started expressing myself through Bollywood dancing on my Instagram page and sharing a deeper insight into my life as a digital entrepreneur. These were all things that I was passionate about, and I was now showing them to the world.

Let me tell you what ended up happening:

Most of my passions have now been converted into individual revenue streams for my business. It took time and consistent effort, but it proved that I didn't have to force myself to choose one passion for being successful. I could be multi-passionate *and* achieve the success defined by me. I'm glad I stuck on to my faith that I would be able to pursue my passions as well as find my success in it.

Here's something that not many people realize:

In this day and age, there is *nothing* you can't monetize. You do not need to have just one passion. Being passionate about something doesn't mean you cannot be passionate about something else.

We live in a fantastic age where you can monetize any and *all* of your passions.

In fact, because you can monetize any and all of your passions, you can create multiple income streams for your business this way. In other words, being multi-passionate actually helps you grow your monetary abundance.

I used to feel restricted about following just one passion, but not anymore. I follow my passions, yes, plural, ***passions***, and I know each one of them doesn't take away from my success but, in fact, contributes to it.

If you're a multi-passionate person, believe me, that is your biggest strength. You get to choose the passions you'd like to pursue. You get to forge your own way to success without feeling restricted.

Just because people know a norm doesn't mean other ways are wrong. It just means these ways are yet to be created and doesn't that sound exciting for you to pursue?

3.9

Is it necessary, or is it shiny?

When I started this entrepreneurial journey, I didn't know what I was doing.

I was implementing what I thought were good strategies to grow my business, but I wasn't really sure if it would work or if I was wasting my time. I had a lot riding on this journey, adding a subconscious layer of fear.

That fear did help me in some ways by motivating me to do better daily.

However, one side effect of the fear was that I caught the Shiny Object Syndrome, and I caught it bad.

The Shiny Object Syndrome, one's tendency to impulsively chase the new and abandon the current, hindered my growth during the initial days.

For example, suppose I was implementing one strategy for my business. I'd see a successful entrepreneur implementing another strategy, and I would abandon my current one to immediately implement the new one that caught my attention.

I was hopping from strategy to strategy without thoroughly implementing one, which meant I wasn't seeing any results. For lack of better words, I'd say I was wasting my time.

If I were to look back now, I guess I was afraid of missing out on the strategies working for other entrepreneurs. I thought that if it worked for them, it would definitely work for me.

It was a vicious cycle and one that I found very, very hard to break.

It came to a point where I would look back and find that my business was stagnant. Stagnant because none of the strategies were implemented long enough for me to see growth.

It was a hard pill for me to swallow when I went through a few months of zero income and no growth on any of my social media platforms. I knew I had to overcome the Shiny Object Syndrome. I wasn't sure where I would even start. The impulse was so fast that most of the time, I wouldn't even realize I was running to the newest thing until it was too late.

Because I couldn't see the impulse, I had to find another way to reel myself back. I thought of introducing a question before I changed strategies. Just a tiny pause where I would ask myself:

Is it necessary, or is it shiny?

My answer was "it is shiny" nine out of ten times. The minute I answered the question, I would feel my impulse reducing. My rational mind would take over and calm my fears of missing out.

I cannot tell you how this simple question has diverted me from making so many bad decisions for my business. It helped me identify which decisions were essential for my business and which could wait.

Another step that has helped me overcome my Shiny Object Syndrome was giving myself a timeline for each strategy I implemented.

For example, if I was trying out a new type of content for Instagram, I would keep a timeline of implementing it for at least ninety days to see if the strategy was working or not. In those ninety days, I would keep posting the same kind of content and implementing one strategy. I wouldn't allow myself to switch over to another strategy until those ninety days were up. Once the ninety days were up and I found a new strategy, I would again ask myself if it was necessary or shiny. Depending on my answer, I would take my next steps.

If you struggle with Shiny Object Syndrome, I recommend trying this method.

Every time you are about to try a new strategy, take a pause and ask yourself the following questions:

- Is it necessary, or is it shiny?

- Am I doing this because I feel pressured or because my business needs it?

- Is it the right time to implement this strategy, or am I rushing this?

Sometimes, you may not have an answer immediately. Wait till you have an answer, and then continue with your next steps.

Better to pause before, than regret after, right?

CHAPTER 4
MARKETING

Make plan ☑
Follow plan ☑
Don't cry ☑

The stable foundation you need.

4.1

Niche down by the Process of Elimination.

In September 2019, I had no idea which services I wanted to offer as a freelancer.

I'd already gotten a freelance job, but I knew I had to clarify my services to get more projects. I wanted to do something in marketing, but I just wasn't sure what. Marketing has over 100 categories, and I was interested in many of them. So, I wrote down all the services I could offer as a marketing freelancer.

I came up with twenty-three services, from email marketing to website creation to blog writing, copywriting, and so on. I was pretty proud of myself.

But that sense of pride was short-lived.

I put all those services on my website and my profile on the freelance platforms. I applied to various posted jobs, but I heard nothing back. As I spoke to potential clients, it became more challenging for me to explain what I did. There wasn't one thing I could be known for, and since I had listed twenty-three services, my entire profile was confusing.

I thought it would be lucrative to potential clients if I had a huge list of services. However, not only was it confusing to my clients, but this list was also starting to overwhelm me.

I soon realized that the services I was offering were too broad for someone just stepping into the entrepreneurial world. I needed to be known for a well-defined marketing section as "marketing" was too broad a spectrum.

As soon as I realized this, I looked at my list to see which ones I really wanted to do.

I chose all.

I sighed. This was not the best way to go about it.

I tried again, and yup, you guessed right, there wasn't a single change in my new list.

Those were all my skills, which I had taken the time and effort to learn. Why did I have to give some of them up? I was indignant.

The list reminded me of the options in exams I took in twelfth grade—or second PUC as it is called in Karnataka, India. We had these state-level competitive exams in which you had 180 questions with four options, all to be answered in 180 minutes.

In these exams, each question was designed so that you didn't need too much time to work it out if you applied the suitable method.

I went for tuitions where I was taught how to determine a suitable method by looking at the question. My tuition teacher had a saying that if it was taking you too long to solve the problem, you were approaching it wrong.

There was one such method called the Process of Elimination. It works as the name suggests.

If you didn't find any unique method to solve the question, you would look at the options and remove the ones that didn't align with the question.

I liked this method. I probably used it a lot more than I should have. I liked this method so much that I started applying it to my life choices.

So, when I didn't know what to do about my marketing services list, I thought the Process of Elimination could help me bring it down to three services.

Right around this time, I got two more freelance jobs. One was to create a website from scratch, and another was blog writing for the website.

They both had a project-based and not a time-based pricing system.

It took me twice the amount of time to create the website. It came out amazing, but it wasn't my core strength. I was getting paid half of my rate for an hour because I hadn't mastered the skill enough for me to make a profit on the project-based payment. In other words, I wasn't an expert at it.

That service was removed from my list using the Process of Elimination. It was a bit heartbreaking because I earned a massive tip from the client for my work, but on the other hand, as I was working on their website, it was clear that I needed more time to master that skill.

The next job was blog writing for a website. I did not like it one bit. I was doing a lot of writing work for my website, and my brain was already at total capacity for writing-related stuff.

While some blog writers can write different kinds of articles for various niches every day and not feel burned out, it was not something I could do. I liked focusing all my attention on one niche with blog writing. This way, I could intertwine them and create a flow. For me, that was where I could weave my magic. I wasn't keen on taking on blog writing for other industries either. I finished the job of five articles and immediately struck that service off my list.

Slowly, one by one, I got short-term jobs to see how I felt about the particular marketing category and took a call on whether to eliminate it or to keep it on the list.

That was the best way for me to go about the whole thing. Given that I was eliminating the items on the list, no part of me second-guessed the decisions I was making. Within eight months, I was able to eliminate twenty items on the list, and eight months after that, I was able to eliminate two more, bringing it down to only one service in January 2021—Marketing Strategy Consulting.

That was also the start of positioning myself as a Marketing Strategy Consultant and establishing myself as an expert in that field. Today, potential clients know what I can help them with, and there is no confusion on either end. It's been simpler to build my identity, keeping one niche in mind rather than twenty-three.

When you're starting out, you have this invariable gush of energy to add in as many products or services as possible. It makes you feel safer, and you're going to argue that you're working to **ALL** your strengths. You fear that if you narrow your focus, you may lose out on potential clients.

When you start with a broad niche, you can't position yourself as an expert. It goes against the very definition of an expert. When you can't position yourself as an expert, it's even more difficult for potential clients to trust you with their work. There's already quite a bit of skepticism regarding work deliverability for digital entrepreneurs because there is no in-person relationship. Your potential client must trust you based on what you portray online, and if you're not an expert, why would they hire you for the job?

As I always say, there's no right or wrong step in the entrepreneurial journey, but there are harder steps and simpler steps.

Having a broader niche makes it harder to establish yourself as the authority in your field. It takes longer to gain your customer's trust, and it gets frustrating when it takes an unnecessarily long time to see the results of your efforts.

The key word is "unnecessary".

If you're just like me and feel emotionally attached to all the sections of your broad niche, then the simple way to go about this would be to use the Process of Elimination. You may not have the time or the opportunity to try out each section of your broad niche just like I did, but you can still imagine what it would be like to work in each section of your broad niche. Eliminate it if it feels off, or you're not going to enjoy the process, or if you feel it may not be your strongest suit.

You can also ask yourself the following:

♦   What is the one thing I wish to be known for?

♦   In which field would I like to be considered an expert?

Use these questions as a starting point to establish yourself as an expert in one niche, and later on, if you want, you can expand your niche.

First, think about how you will grow from a small fish to a big fish in a small pond, and then later, you can think about how you'll adapt in a bigger pond.

As much as we'd love to be the bigger fish, wasn't the bigger fish once a small fish too?

If you visit www.themarketingnomad.co/zero-to-four-figures, you'll get access to a printable workbook with a step-by-step process to help you figure out your niche.

4.2

The simplest way to start your marketing: Create paths to find you.

Despite being a marketer with an MBA and work experience, I found it overwhelming to set up marketing strategies for my business.

When I started in September 2019, I was eager to use everything I had learned. There were so many strategies that I went dizzy trying to analyze which ones to use for my business. The marketer in me started with all the complex marketing that I had learned. After a couple of those marketing strategies backfired on me, I realized that all those marketing strategies needed one collective starting point before they could be implemented.

So, I put a pin in all the complex marketing strategies I wanted to implement for my business. Those were not meant for Level Zero, and I was at Level Zero. There would come a time when I would slowly start adding those in, just not right now.

This was around December 2019. I focused on just one thing: creating paths for people to find me. That was it.

If you look at every action I have taken since I started my business, this tactic of mine shines through.

I set up my website because I wanted it to be one way for people to find me.

I started writing blog posts on my website because that was another path for people to find me.

I started an Instagram page dedicated to The Marketing Nomad because, you guessed it, it was a path for people to find me.

The same goes for my YouTube channel, podcast, Etsy digital shop and Skillshare class.

As traffic increased on these paths, I could add complex marketing strategies to further increase the traffic.

For example, in my blog posts, if I was talking about Instagram marketing and I had a similar podcast episode on Instagram marketing, I would add a link to the podcast episode in the blog post.

With my Etsy digital shop, I created strategies that would lead people to my other platforms and encourage my customers to look at my other products.

With my Instagram page, I created a lead magnet funnel. I made a link to more paths leading to my other resources through my YouTube channel. Soon, every path of mine was interlinked, and I could keep adding more strategies to strengthen each path.

Even now, when I look at my marketing, it all boils down to me creating paths for people to find me and strengthening each of those paths. I'd love to give you fancy names for the marketing strategies I'm using, but if I have to summarize my entire marketing in five words, it would be this:

Creating Paths to Find Me.

If you'd like to implement this lesson for your business, here's how you can go about it:

♦ Look at where your audience hangs out and see how you can create a path from their point to you.

- Do the same step for the other platforms you choose. Interlink each of those paths as best as you can. This allows people to stay longer on the paths leading to you. The longer they remain on your paths, the lower the chances of wandering off to your competitors' paths.

- Over time, build on the strength of these paths with additional marketing strategies. After you've set up your paths, you'll better understand what marketing strategies you could use to improve the traffic on the paths. There's always trial and error, or you could hire a marketing strategy consultant like me to help you. *wink*

There will be many marketing strategies you can implement, but wouldn't you want to start with the one that can help you tie your future marketing efforts together?

Visit www.themarketingnomad.co/zero-to-four-figures to get access to a printable workbook to create paths for your business.

4.3

Tell everyone.

One of the first things I did as a digital entrepreneur was to show up on my personal social media pages and announce the change in my career path.

I wrote a post on LinkedIn and said I was starting this journey. I changed my profile banner to list the marketing services I offered. I did the same on my personal Instagram account and my personal Facebook account too.

My mom took things a step further.

She told everyone she met that I was now a marketing freelancer and had my own website with my services listed.

Now first off, let me clarify something. My mom wasn't telling them to boast about me.

My mom is a typical Indian parent. If I got 98/100 in a math exam, she'd ask me where I lost the two marks. When I had to learn a duet dance to perform in front of 5,000 people for the 75th Anniversary Celebrations in 2003 for D.A.V Hindi School (Singapore), my mom was there at every practice session. She worked with me to fix every mistake I made just so I would be perfect for my performance. It even came down to her helping me match my dance step to the exact beat of the music. She would always say "pause" so

I would slow down my pace to match the beat. *(I rocked that performance, which remains one of my most precious memories.)*

My point is that my mom has always looked for areas of improvement rather than what's already perfected. It's a trait of hers that I've grown to understand and appreciate.

So, when she told everyone about me, it was more to let them know that they could contact me if they needed my services or knew someone who needed marketing help.

In all honesty, when she would tell them, I'd be standing there awkwardly and giving a sheepish smile. I found it incredibly embarrassing. I didn't think anyone other than business owners would be interested to know about my marketing services.

When I'd protest, she'd say, *"You never know where your clients will come from, Chinna[6]."*

I didn't understand it at all.

Six months later, someone contacted me asking for more information about my marketing services. When I asked them how they found me, they said one of my mom's friends mentioned me.

That was a very humbling moment for me.

I did not expect someone who hadn't used my services to be talking about me. It did not even occur to me that that could happen.

As a marketer, I knew the power of word-of-mouth marketing. However, word-of-mouth marketing usually happens *after* someone has used your products or services. For example, if a client referred me to someone else, that would be word-of-mouth marketing, and I did have a few of those. I didn't think people could talk about my services when they had no

---

[6] It's my mom's pet name for me. It means "gold" in Kannada.

connection to what I did.

It was at that moment that I realized the power of telling every single person. My mom was right! It was true.

You never really know where your next client or customer will come from. All you can do is make sure everyone around you knows what you do and what you can offer.

After learning that lesson, I also told everyone that I was now a digital entrepreneur and mentioned the marketing services I offered. There were no longer any exceptions. I told everyone.

As entrepreneurs and business owners, we often overlook the people in our existing network. We try to reach out to people we don't know. Maybe there's an innate fear that the people we know may think differently of us if we talk to them about our services. Or maybe, there's a tad bit of emotional investment when we tell people in our existing network. Some of us may feel that if we don't tell our existing network, it won't disappoint us if they don't refer us.

But here's what I've learned:

You don't have to restrict talking about your services with only the people who are a fit for your business.

Talking about your services to your existing network doesn't mean you expect them to help you out. They aren't obligated to, and we'll talk more about this in the Relationships chapter [Section 7.4].

They may or may not be actively thinking of helping you. Everyone has a busy life. But that doesn't rule out that they may remember your services when they want to help someone else looking for you.

Sometimes, you may feel stumped about how to talk about your services with people who may not be connected to your field. Don't worry; here's a simple and easy-to-remember template for you:

Hi! I've started on my own and am a _____ *(designation)*. I help _____ *(target audience)* to _____ *(service)*. For example, if _____ *(explain the problem your target audience faces)*, then I step in and _____ *(how you would fix the problem)* to _____ *(transformation)*. If you hear someone asking about _____ or _____ *(keywords related to your field)*, please send them my way!

The last sentence is important because people may or may not remember what you do, but they will remember the keywords connected to you. That's a tiny marketing tactic that I use. **wink**

This would be my version as a Marketing Strategy Consultant:

"Hi! I've started on my own and am a <u>Marketing Strategy Consultant</u>. I help <u>business owners and solopreneurs</u> to <u>implement marketing strategies to grow their businesses</u>. For example, if <u>they want to launch their product soon</u>, then I step in and <u>help them plan what to do on social media to increase their launch sales</u>. If you hear someone asking about <u>marketing</u> or <u>social media</u>, please send them my way!"

It helps to practice this in front of a mirror until you are comfortable talking about yourself and your services. Another tip would be to break down what you do into common person language instead of adding industry jargon. If it is simple for people to understand what you do, it is easier for them to recommend you.

And of course, my question to end this section would be, who would you like to start telling today?

4.4

It's all about positioning.

About three months into my journey, I knew it was time to set up my dedicated social media profiles for "The Marketing Nomad".

I was able to get a few jobs from the freelance platforms but getting outbid 99% of the time was really getting to me. I wanted the freedom to set my own pricing and knew I couldn't do it without any social media backing.

As a marketer, I understood the power of social media. According to an article I read for one of my marketing classes during my MBA program, "Reviewing and Conceptualizing Customer-Perceived Value"[7], customer value is preferential and relativistic. That meant, for me to get more jobs at the price point I wished, my potential customers had to *prefer* my services over others.

Thus began my official marketing work for my personal brand. Now at this point, there was a really different move I made that propelled my personal brand. Instead of listing out reasons my potential customers would prefer me over my competitors, I dug deeper and asked myself what *I* wanted those reasons to be. For aspirational reasons or for reasons that already existed, I

---

[7] Chang, et al. "Reviewing and conceptualizing customer-perceived value." *The Marketing Review* 12.3 (2012): 253-274.

looked inward and allowed myself to have control over their perception of my services.

By doing this, I was able to see how I could be my potential customers' preference while staying true to myself. My list was now a healthy balance of my preference and theirs.

After making my list, I began listing actions I needed to take to balance both preferences.

For example, if I wanted to be seen as an expert by my potential customers, I had to give marketing tips on my social media platforms.

I didn't stop there. Over the next few months, if there was a gap between how I desired to be perceived and how my potential customers perceived me, I would add action items to bridge the gap. For example, if I wanted my potential customers to trust me more, I would start opening up more about my life and share what I was up to behind the scenes. These steps really helped me strengthen my personal brand to where it is today. Any platform you find me on, my personal brand is how *I* want to be perceived, and each step of positioning myself has been highly intentional.

As digital entrepreneurs, we often forget that we have a choice in who we attract as clients or customers. Especially when I started out, some of the projects I got weren't aligned with what I wanted to do.

This was on me. I wasn't clear about why I wanted my potential customers/clients to choose my services over others. That led to me leaving money on the table because my potential clients were choosing other services over mine.

This wasn't because I was not good, but because I had failed to position myself correctly.

At the end of the day, you could be the expert in your field. You could have multiple degrees. You could have a ton of work experience. But if you aren't able to position yourself to show the value of all that you bring to the table, your audience won't be able to see it.

Here are a few questions to help you position yourself:

- ◆ How do I want to be perceived by my potential clients?

- ◆ How do I want to be perceived by my existing clients?

- ◆ What are three things that I'd like to stand out with? Am I currently aligned with those three things? If not, then what steps can I take to align with those?

- ◆ What are five reasons I would like my clients to prefer me over my competitors?

- ◆ *(After a few months of intentional positioning)* How do my potential clients perceive me now? Is there a gap between how they perceive me and how I would like to be perceived? Why do I think the gap exists? What are some actionable steps I can take to bridge that gap?

Even when you aren't actively positioning yourself, that is positioning by itself though it will not be in alignment with what you want. Positioning in alignment with what you want is a conscious effort and requires constant evaluation. Believe it or not, a considerable part of your success relies on how aligned your positioning is to your aim.

How you position is what people see, so doesn't it help to position yourself the way *you'd* like to be seen?

Visit www.themarketingnomad.co/zero-to-four-figures to get access to a printable workbook to help you position yourself.

4.5

Plan your content schedule to the time you have on hand.

As a marketer at a full-time job in 2018, I spent a reasonable amount of time on content creation.

I would design content like social media posts, marketing collateral to help salespeople on their sales calls, ads for magazines, and even billboards for local events. Content creation was a big part of my job description, so naturally, much of my daily attention was focused on it.

I continued viewing myself as a marketer for the first few months of my entrepreneurial journey. I focused heavily on content creation and marketing efforts for my personal brand. This worked well for a while. I only had a few clients, so I had a lot of time.

However, in August 2020, when things started picking up for my business, I was hard-pressed for time. It became difficult for me to balance all my activities. The marketer instinct in me refused to reduce my hours of content creation and other marketing activities. Instead, I tried cramming my other business-related activities into whatever little time I had left.

As you may have already guessed, the time I had left was just not enough. I was now a business owner and not just a marketer. Along with that title came a whole horde of responsibilities and tasks—administrative work, client work, etc. As much as marketing and content creation was necessary for my business, they could no longer take a majority of my time.

For me, the mindset shifts from being a marketer to a business owner happened in stages. Deep down, it was ingrained that marketing was my bread and butter. I had to unlearn this thought process and learn that as a business owner, my tasks were much more than just marketing.

Once I recognized the number of tasks I had as a business owner, I knew my method of completing those tasks was flawed. I focused heavily on marketing, even though there were other tasks of higher priority.

I had to find a better way to do my tasks according to priority.

So, I listed out all my tasks. From filing for taxes to managing the backend administrative functions of my company to sending out proposals, to actual client work, to content creation, to email marketing, I wrote it all.

I then started prioritizing those tasks from the view of a business owner and not a marketer. I also approximated how much time I would need for each weekly task. Since I used to spend most of my time on content creation, it was not surprising that I spent more hours on it than on the rest of the tasks.

I only had twenty-four hours a day, and it seemed impossible to fit everything. I could have hired someone, but at the stage I was, I knew I couldn't afford it. I was almost there, but just not yet.

I looked at my list again. The amount of time I had put into content creation seemed to be throwing everything off balance. I scratched off the number of hours I had written beside it. I then calculated how much time all the other tasks would add. When I subtracted how much time I needed to sleep, rest, do self-care, keep for personal commitments, etc., I was left with around three hours per week. I kept that amount of time for my content creation.

It wasn't that simple implementing this, though. My previous content creation process took much more than three hours a week. Of course, this was because the content I was creating was intensive. Now that I only had three hours a week to make all my content, I needed to change the content to ensure I could fit it all in three hours a week.

For example, if my reels on Instagram took one hour to create for the week, I changed the content so that it would take me only thirty minutes to create for the entire week.

At this time, I was doing a lot of podcast interviews hosting guests, which took nearly two-three hours of my time every week. After rearranging my time, I realized I could not afford to give that amount of time every week. So, I streamlined my guest interview processes to fit the time I had on hand. Not just that, I also reduced the frequency of my episodes.

I also did the same with my YouTube channel. Each YouTube video took me a lot of time to create. It was taking me that long because I had scripted every sentence of mine, making me feel very restricted. I would keep reshooting every other sentence because I kept going off-script. Around this time, I was also recovering from my massive burnout, and as I mentioned earlier, I realized that my biggest strength was my love for talking freely. I knew I needed to focus on that. I stopped scripting my YouTube videos in detail and kept only five minutes for scripting each video. I listed the main points, and the rest was all on-spot talking, which I absolutely loved. My episodes took significantly lesser time to shoot and edit now.

I wouldn't have made these radical shifts in my content creation process if I hadn't planned my content creation time according to the time I had left. Using this planning method, I could balance my tasks as a business owner and a marketer. I would call this one of the best strategic shifts I've made in my business. This move instigated a more rapid growth of my business.

Over the following months, I could afford to hire independent contractors to help me with specific tasks. That freed up some of my time, and I would increase my content creation time accordingly. Other times, there would be an increase in my responsibilities as a business owner, and I would adjust my content creation time to suit my needs.

One of the most frequently asked questions by my clients who are solopreneurs is, "*How much time should I dedicate to content creation?*"

Here's my answer: Content creation is *one* part of the wheel and not the whole wheel that runs your business.

There is a significant emphasis on content creation in the digital entrepreneurial world, so I understand why solopreneurs feel pressured to give all their time to content creation when content creation should only be one part of their business activities.

Another problem I have noticed with solopreneurs is the lack of consistency in their content creation.

It becomes easier to stay consistent when you plan your content creation according to the time you have left. You've already prioritized your other tasks and given them the needed time. Now, you have a realistic duration for your content creation process, and it becomes easier to keep up with it long-term.

Here's how you can use my Remainder Content Creation (RCC) Method to plan your content creation:

Step 1: List all your tasks for a week or a month.

Step 2: List out your personal commitments.

Step 3: Write how much time it takes for you to complete every other task on your list.

Step 4: Subtract it from the total number of hours you have in that time frame.

Step 5: Realistically determine how much content you can create in the time you have left.

Step 6: Determine the frequency of your content from the amount of content you can create. For example, in the time that you have left, if you can record, edit, and upload one podcast episode per week, that would be your frequency.

Your page should look something like this:

DURATION: One Week – 168 Hours		
TASKS	HOURS	TIME LEFT
Tax filing	5	17
Sending out proposals	4	13
Stats tracking	3	10
add more tasks	5	**5**

CONTENT CREATION TASKS	TIME TAKEN	TIME LEFT	FREQ.
Podcast record, edit, upload	1.5	3.5	1
IG reels – create, edit, upload	2	1.5	3
Blog post	1.5	0	1

If you are a business owner who does all your tasks, including content creation, I highly recommend this method to help you balance your time better. This method enables you to prioritize your tasks and helps you understand how to make the best use of your time as a business owner.

Better plan, lesser overwhelm, right?

Visit www.themarketingnomad.co/zero-to-four-figures to get access to a printable workbook to help you implement this strategy for your content creation.

4.6

·

Learn to detach from your products/services.

When I started my membership program in September 2020, it aimed to help business owners, entrepreneurs, and solopreneurs with their long-term marketing efforts.

It had monthly course content to provide marketing help to business owners and entrepreneurs. I had a live Q and A session for about thirty to forty minutes each month. I also had group sessions where each member would talk about what they were currently struggling with, and all of us on the video call would brainstorm ideas to help each other out.

The amount of time I was investing in the membership program was extensive. Unfortunately, despite the forty people joining in during the product launch, the revenue coming in from the program was not enough to help me sustain it long-term. As much as I loved helping my members, I needed to make a certain revenue from the membership program for it to make financial sense, and I couldn't.

In July 2021, I made the painful decision to end my membership program by September 2021. When I started, I told my members I would try the program for a year. I really thought I could keep it going even longer than that. It was heartbreaking to tell them that I needed to end the membership program soon.

Coming to this decision was not easy. I mulled over the decision for two to three months before that. I was too attached to the product as I had invested so much time and effort. I loved the bi-weekly interactions with my members. I enjoyed every minute I spent working on my membership program. I did not want to end it at all. If money was out of the equation, I would have continued with no hesitation.

But money was a part of the equation. As much as I wanted to keep it going, my business could not support the product financially.

I would always call myself a business owner, but the day I had to make that decision, I began to *see* myself as a business owner. The weight and responsibility of making that decision made me realize that I must never take my role as a business owner lightly.

There were a couple more situations after that incident where I had to ignore what I wanted to do and put my company's needs first.

One incident was a client requesting the revision of the project's price according to their budget. I really wanted to work on this project, and I knew that the client was fantastic to work with.

I would have revised the pricing in a heartbeat if it were up to me.

But it wasn't up to me.

I had to weigh the pros and cons from my business' perspective. Anything less than the price point I had given for the project's duration wouldn't have been financially viable for my business.

So, I couldn't reduce the price point for the same level of engagement. That was another big reminder that I was now a business owner and that each decision had to be what was best for my business.

Instead, I provided different levels of engagement at various price points and gave the decision flexibility to my client. I could work around my client's budget, but I couldn't reduce the prices for the same number of services.

This way, regardless of what my client chose, their choice would be a financially viable option for my business.

When we, as entrepreneurs and business owners, create our products/services, we're heavily invested emotionally, mentally, and physically in the process. Whether we like it or not, we form an attachment with our products/services. We're only human. But what you want to do comes secondary when you are an entrepreneur/business owner. The needs of your business come first.

Here are a few questions to help you detach from your product/service and objectively let you know if it is time to ax your product/service or keep it going:

♦ Is the return on investment for my time, resources, etc., worth it?

♦ Am I over-investing my time into the product? Can I cut back on my time and resource investment for the product? If yes, will it be financially viable then?

♦ Is it just one bad month, or has it been a prolonged non-performance?

♦ Have I exhausted all methods to improve the sales of the product/service?

♦ Does the product/service need to be removed entirely, or can it be tweaked instead?

As entrepreneurs and business owners, it's not easy to detach from something we've created with love and passion. But we have to realize that it is only through detachment that our business can really progress.

And progress is what we all are working towards, aren't we?

4.7

Keep one goal per platform.

When I entered the online world as an entrepreneur, there were a plethora of digital platforms for me to choose from.

As I mentioned earlier, the third step to becoming a digital entrepreneur was to create paths for people to find me or my products. As a digital entrepreneur, I wanted these platforms to be online.

When I started, the platforms I chose were—a blog on my website, Instagram, and YouTube. My audience searched for my products on these platforms, so I set camp there.

In the beginning, my only goal was to get leads. That was it.

Regardless of the platform, my goal was to get people interested in my products and services. Given that each digital platform had the same goal, I would repurpose my content on these three platforms.

If I wrote a blog post on "Three Ways to Grow Your Instagram Account", I would create a carousel post for Instagram with the exact same points. I would also make a YouTube video with the same tips.

After almost two years of doing this, it got a bit monotonous for me.

As a marketer, I knew the power of repurposing content. Still, there was also this nagging feeling that I was not wholly utilizing the potential of these platforms for my business.

As a business owner who was seeing a little bit of success by this time, I knew I had to look at new ways to grow my business with the limited amount of time I had each day. I wanted to find ways to get more done with the same effort.

Over time, I realized, repurposing or not, there was still a time investment on my end to create content for each of these platforms. Instead of keeping the same goal for each of the platforms, I decided to have one goal for each platform.

I listed out different goals that my business needed to hit. There was brand awareness, there was lead generation, establishing my authority as an industry leader, there was increasing brand engagement, and lastly, there was also improving my SEO.

My blog took the role of improving my SEO. I decided to keep the goal of lead generation for my website. For brand awareness, I chose YouTube. For brand engagement, I chose Instagram. To establish my authority as an industry leader, I decided on Podcast.

Now I just want to point out that the platforms you choose for your business can differ from mine. The goals you choose for each of these platforms can be different too.

I changed the content in each platform to match their respective goals. It was quite the dramatic shift, and full disclosure, I did lose a few followers/subscribers when I changed my strategy. That kind of follower/subscriber loss is expected because people would be following you for a particular type of content, and when you change it, they may or may not like it. If it doesn't align with their needs, they will naturally unfollow/unsubscribe.

I knew this would happen, so I wasn't worried. I was confident that my new kind of content would help my business better. I also knew the variety in my content from different platforms would attract the type of audience who aligned better with my brand.

Within two months of keeping a specific goal per platform, I started to see different results with almost the same amount of time investment on my end. I say "almost" because there was an additional time investment to script for one more platform. I'd like to add that by this time, my scripts were only a few sentences long, so they didn't take too much time.

I was hitting different marketing goals, and it was amazing to see how all of it was coming together to help my business grow.

I'm not going to go into detail about how I create content for each of these platforms as that gets a little marketing heavy and I want to keep this book a little light on the technical side. *(Maybe my next book? *wink*)*

My point is, as a digital entrepreneur or an online business owner, you get various platforms to choose from. If done right, each of those platforms can help you hit different goals for your business. Especially if you're the only one working for your business right now, it's pretty challenging to get more done with the same effort or time on your end. This has worked well for me and having different goals for each platform has helped me track my progress as a business too.

I also want to add that just because one platform has one goal doesn't mean it's not helping you with another goal.

For example, even though the primary goal for my YouTube channel is to help me with brand awareness, it does drive traffic to my Etsy shop. In marketing, we call this lead generation. In other words, my YouTube channel also helps with lead generation.

But the primary goal of my YouTube channel is brand awareness, and all my content is aimed at helping my YouTube channel bring more brand awareness to The Marketing Nomad. Lead generation is a by-product of that primary goal, not its main goal.

I wish I had done this sooner and not waited two years to make this shift.

Here are a few questions you can ask yourself while you're setting up your platforms:

♦ What are my marketing goals? *(Example: Lead generation, brand awareness, nurturing existing customers, increasing website traffic, etc.)*

♦ What are my platforms?

♦ Which marketing goal suits the platform I have chosen?

♦ What kind of content aligns with that marketing goal? Does it align with the platform as well?

Your page should look something like this:

MARKETING GOAL	PLATFORM	CONTENT
Brand Awareness	*Blog*	*Answers to FAQs, SEO friendly content*
Lead Generation	*Instagram*	*Transformation from product, reviews*

I also want to mention that if you're more comfortable keeping the same goal for all platforms, then go for it. I added this lesson because this was a significant strategic move I made for my business, and I'd like to give you another option for your marketing strategy for digital platforms.

Now that you've got one more way to approach your marketing, which one suits your business best?

Visit www.themarketingnomad.co/zero-to-four-figures to get access to a printable workbook to help you plan your goals and content for each platform.

CHAPTER 5
GROWTH MINDSET

Ready ✔

Set ✔

Grow ✔

Where you water, blossoms.

5.1

Start with a higher purpose.

When I started as a freelancer in my first year, my sole purpose was to see if this was something I could sustain long-term.

In December 2019, I had a clear defining moment that made me confirm I could sustain this long-term. Let's rewind a bit.

In September 2019, with my first client from a freelance platform, I was getting paid $250/month for twelve hours of work per week, and the contract was for four months.

I got the job through a job posting on a freelance platform, and you need to place a bid on these platforms. Most of the time, the lowest bid gets picked. The lowest for this job was $2 an hour, and mine was the highest bid at $5 an hour.

I still got picked, and I was glad. Even though $5 an hour was not the going rate for someone who had an MBA degree, I was grateful for the job. At least I was earning something in my first month, making me feel I was starting somewhere instead of at ground zero.

I thought it would be equally easy for me to get more clients. I did get one or two clients after, but that was it.

Post-November 2019, I didn't get any new clients. One week went by. Two. Then three.

Nothing. Nada. Not even a whisper.

I started getting desperate. Even though some of the jobs posted were not what I wanted to do, I still bid on them, and every time, I got outbid.

Around this time, I started looking for advice on how to grow organically. I looked at how other freelancers earned five or six figures per month. All the online advice was very generic or difficult for me to implement as a broke freelancer.

Even the marketing and business advice available on the internet was not practical at all. They were just the kind where you get quick results, but those results were not healthy for long-term implementation.

I was starting to get frustrated with the lack of appropriate content for new entrepreneurs and business owners. Content that was solid, practical, and could be implemented long-term without burning a massive hole in one's pocket.

Through this frustration, I decided it was going to be my mission to educate and empower business owners worldwide to confidently implement long-term and actionable strategies.

This was my defining moment. I found my higher purpose.

No longer was I concerned about myself.

Instead of asking myself, *"How will I get a new client this month?"* I started asking myself, *"How do I make the lives of business owners better? How can I contribute? What can I do to make them feel confident?"*

The more I started to project my questions about making a difference, the clearer my path became. I started "The Marketing Nomad" Instagram page to share my journey so other business owners and entrepreneurs would feel supported. This was Dec 7, 2019.

Every action I have taken since has been to fulfill my higher purpose.

I set up my company in Delaware, USA soon after, in the middle of a pandemic in August 2020, because I knew that regardless of how this journey would pan out, I wanted to help as many businesses as possible. I couldn't do it unless I had a legit company backing me for various legal and practical reasons.

People ask me how I have managed to do so much in such a short time, and I genuinely believe I've been able to do so because my higher purpose is not about earning money for myself but about making a difference to business owners around me in as many ways as possible.

Frankly, the thought of even writing this book wouldn't have come to my mind if I wasn't aligned with a higher purpose. I mean, tell me, honestly, have you ever seen anyone writing a whole book about how they got to four figures? Well, not yet at least.

But here this book is, in your hands, because I know how arduous my journey has been until now. I know the drastic shifts I had to make in my approach, and by sharing it with you, I hope to make your life a little bit easier.

To be honest, I have a million reasons why I shouldn't move forward with this book.

Reasons like—I don't have a publisher. No one's written a book like this. I will be using my entire savings to get this out to you. I haven't done this before. And so on and so forth.

Regardless of how many reasons I could use to stop writing, I'm still going to do it because it serves my higher purpose.

Having a higher purpose also motivates me every single day. Whether it is to create videos or spend time editing them, record podcasts, or show up on various other platforms, I spend a lot of energy helping business owners across the world. Still, I really wouldn't have it any other way.

I know it is absolutely worth it because I'm making a difference to at least one business owner. I know that just by showing up, I'm creating a reality where business owners are confident in their journey.

Yes, I do have my own responsibilities. I do have my dreams that I hope to achieve from my entrepreneurial journey, but having a higher purpose, a purpose which is beyond me, adds meaning to what I do, and *that* changes how I show up for my business.

Of the 5% of my clients still on their entrepreneurial journey, one crucial factor was common to all of them. I probably sound like a teacher when I say this, but I ask this question to every single client I work with:

"Why do you do what you do?"

This is always the first question I ask, and it is more so for me to understand where they want to take their business and how I can create marketing strategies that align with their purpose.

The ones who continued their entrepreneurial journey had one thing in common—they, too, had a higher purpose and mission behind their business.

I believe the entrepreneurial journey is fundamentally about making a difference to the people around you.

You may have other reasons like helping yourself gain financial freedom/independence, making ends meet, paying off your debt, etc., but these are reasons that center around you.

There's nothing wrong with having those reasons, but those aren't enough to fuel you as you venture deeper on this path.

When you see your business only as a way to help yourself, you'll work on it for a while before realizing you can do the same while working for someone else. So, you're more likely to give up around the one-year mark, mainly because things take-off slowly during this period.

I just want to say there's nothing wrong with quitting this journey or working for someone. I worked at a fantastic company for a year and loved every minute.

But I'm guessing that when you want to start something on your own, you have some hope of continuing that path. No one begins the entrepreneurial journey with the hopes of quitting it within a year or two.

When you see your business as a way to help the people around you, regardless of how tough things may seem, you're more inclined to keep going.

The reason is simple: You now have a sense of purpose driving you.

When you think about quitting, you realize you must consider the people around you.

The consequence of your decision weighs a lot more when you have a higher purpose. You realize that if you give up, you're not only giving up on your dreams, but you're also giving up on a reality that could have made a difference to the people around you.

You're likely to try every avenue when the consequences weigh more. These avenues may or may not work out, and you may decide to quit the entrepreneurial journey anyway.

The important thing is that you would be more willing to go an extra length to see if you can continue this journey.

There is something that comes out of trying every single avenue—The chances of something clicking increases significantly.

This journey is hard. There will be days when you wake up and ask yourself why you're working so hard. You'll question if you even want to work that hard.

You need to have an answer for yourself.

Don't underestimate how much your sense of higher purpose will keep you motivated through this journey.

So, my friend, tell me, why do you do what you do?

5.2

Place of Insecurity vs. Place of Power—Always, always, always choose the latter.

During my late teens and early twenties, I was really insecure that I wasn't worthy of love.

I know, absolutely heartbreaking.

I didn't think I deserved love, and that entire time of my life was extremely challenging because of my insecurity. I kept allowing people to mistreat me. I had no boundaries. I would chase after people thinking that that was what friendship or love was. The entire period drained me completely, and by the time I was twenty-three, my emotional health had deteriorated significantly.

When I went to Rochester for my MBA program, I thought it could be my chance at a fresh start.

I knew I needed to find a way to overcome my insecurity, or else I would continue sabotaging my emotional and mental health.

During the two years of my time at Rochester, I slowly dug into my insecurities. I started understanding the incidents that triggered each of them. Over time, I could discern my insecurities stemmed from my takeaways from the origin incident.

My takeaway.

My thoughts.

My perception.

The word "my" felt comfortable to me.

If the insecurities came from my perception, then all I had to do was change how I viewed things.

I stopped blaming the people around me and started taking a hard look at my thought process.

Yes, it sucked when the origin incident happened, and the insecurity that came out of it was horrible. But I was older now and had more experience. I also had more control over my thoughts. That meant I could enable myself to see things in a different light.

So, I started working toward changing my perception. My feeling of unworthiness for love was the first insecurity that I consciously tried to work on.

While working on my insecurities, I came up with a concept to better understand my actions. Let me explain it to you.

PLACE OF INSECURITY VS. PLACE OF POWER

After years and years of observing my behavior as well as the behaviors of people around me, I've come to realize that all of one's actions can be divided into two buckets:

1. Place of Power

2. Place of Insecurity

Now let's talk about what each of these means.

Place of Power

When your actions come from a Place of Power, there's usually a positive feeling around it. For lack of a better phrase, you feel in your power.

You are confident about your decision.

You feel stable.

You recognize everything is balanced.

That's also why I named it Place of Power. I wasn't feeling particularly creative that day to call it anything else.

Now let me explain what "positive" feelings are. There's a common misconception that positive feelings just mean happiness. Positive feelings are actually feelings that are natural for you to feel and are a positive influence on your life.

Anger in moderation is actually good for you. The same goes for sadness. Happiness in moderation too. These are all positive emotions when experienced in moderation. When you feel these emotions in moderation, it doesn't leave you feeling uneasy or uncomfortable.

When you express your anger in a healthy way, it makes you feel better.

When you've expressed your sadness in a healthy way, again, it actually brings relief to you.

These emotions are necessary for you to live a healthy and enriching life.

Place of Insecurity

When you are in a Place of Insecurity, you will feel things spinning out of control around you. You won't feel in your element, and something will feel off. There is also a high chance that the actions you take from this place will have more adverse consequences on your life than favorable ones.

You also experience negative emotions. Negative emotions are emotions that leave you feeling uncomfortable, and they drain your energy. Frustration, overwhelm, stress, jealousy, and insecurity are all examples of negative emotions.

It doesn't feel good when you feel any of these emotions, regardless of the capacity.

Every single action from anyone can either be placed into a Place of Power or a Place of Insecurity.

Take a pause from reading this book and think about every action you've taken to date. You'll realize it either falls into a Place of Power or a Place of Insecurity.

Once I had come up with this concept—around the age of twenty-four or twenty-five—I started evaluating every decision of mine.

If I was going to take any action, I asked myself, *"Am I coming from a Place of Power, or am I coming from a Place of Insecurity?"*

It was through this simple question that I could take actions that were more aligned with myself when it came to overcoming my insecurities.

Let's take the insecurity I mentioned earlier—I didn't feel I deserved love.

Over the years to come, through many painstaking efforts and constantly asking myself this simple question, I was able to build healthy boundaries. I found the courage to let people know what was acceptable to me and what wasn't. I no longer begged nor chased anyone. I felt in control of my life.

During this time, there were a lot of fights and anger directed toward me by some of the people I had set healthy boundaries with. But here's the thing about being in a Place of Power—it doesn't matter.

The consequences don't matter to you when you are in a Place of Power because you know what you are doing is the right action for you.

When I started my entrepreneurial journey, I felt a lot of insecurities come up. Given that I had a process to handle my insecurities for my personal relationships, I wondered if I could apply the same to my business-related insecurities. To my surprise, I could!

Let me give you an example of how an insecurity affected the way I showed up for my business and how I applied this concept to overcome it. During the first two years of my entrepreneurial journey, I've had seven product launches. *(This stat does not count the products released in my Etsy digital shop).* Six of these products were mini-courses, and the seventh was a membership program.

For the first product launch in March 2020, I was insecure that no one would buy from me. At the time, I had 300 followers on Instagram.

Being the marketer that I am, I planned the entire launch. This was my area of expertise, and I knew exactly how to go about it. It was going to be a ten-day launch, and I had planned the marketing-related activities for each day of the launch. I even designed the Instagram posts for the entire period.

I felt pretty proud of myself.

However, I stopped promoting after three days.

Yeah, talk about a plot twist.

I ended the launch prematurely because I felt I was being "realistic" and that no one was going to buy anyway.

After a few days, I started to feel uncomfortable. I wasn't sure of my decision at all. I was worried about the consequences of my actions, wondering if I had left money on the table.

The minute I started feeling this way, it was clear that the action I had taken was from a Place of Insecurity. I implemented my framework for overcoming insecurities and found that I was insecure about the number of followers I had on Instagram. Mine wasn't a big account, and I knew there was a considerable possibility of no one buying my product by the end of the launch. I was afraid to face that.

Once I worked through these insecurities, I recognized my mistake. For my next launch, I made sure I stuck out for the entire launch. Regardless of whether I had any responses, I kept promoting until the launch's intended last day.

Not just that, I also reached out to people in my DMs and let them know I had a new product available. I showed up on my Instagram stories every day and was fearless in talking about my products, their benefits, and the transformation that my audience could expect from my product.

No one bought my product for that launch either, but on the last day, I had two inquiries—which was pretty awesome for me given the tiny size of my social media following.

Even though those two inquiries were not ready for my second product, they did move forward with buying my seventh product, which was a win in the end.

I worked from a Place of Power during the subsequent few launches.

It didn't matter whether I would make any sales or not. All that mattered was that I was selling a product that could ease the lives of other business owners, and I had to talk about it.

For each launch, I enjoyed the process and felt more and more in my power.

And that happens when you work from a Place of Power. Regardless of the consequences, you feel confident and in control.

Now let's talk about my framework for moving away from a Place of Insecurity and into a Place of Power.

Step 1: Recognizing the Insecurity

This is probably the most challenging step, and it does take some time to evaluate how you're feeling.

Each time you try to justify your actions to yourself, it's a strong sign that you are coming from a Place of Insecurity.

For example, in the personal example I gave you, even though my actions from the Place of Insecurity led to a lot of overwhelm and frustration, I justified my actions by telling myself that that was how friendship or love was meant to be.

With my business example, even though something did not sit right with me, I justified to myself that I was being "realistic".

For this step, journaling helps detangle what's on your mind and objectively evaluate your thought processes/actions.

A few questions you can try to answer during your journaling practice would be:

- ♦ What am I feeling?

- ♦ Why am I convincing myself to feel a different way?

- ♦ Why don't I feel what I'm supposed to feel?

- ♦ What current perception of myself led me to take this action?

♦ What perception should I have of myself to align with what I want to feel?

Step 2: Visualize

This step is about visualizing the person you would be if you acted from a Place of Power.

For the personal-related example, when I envisioned myself coming from a Place of Power, I realized that my Place of Power version did not allow people to mistreat her. She kept healthy boundaries. She felt confident in expressing her feelings. She would not be worried about the consequences of her actions, even if it meant some people leaving her life.

Once I could envision the person I would be when I was acting from my Place of Power, it became easier for me to implement those steps.

Here's why:

When you start to visualize yourself being in a Place of Power, you get a taste of all the positive emotions you feel when you act from a Place of Power. Once you feel that, you never want to let it go. You will do anything to make sure you continue feeling positive.

That's what happened to me. I visualized how my life would look when I was in control of it and felt every positive emotion flowing through me. Before I knew it, I was setting healthy boundaries. I was removing people who did not align with my life's vision. I was communicating my feelings in a healthy way. I no longer feared telling people what was and wasn't acceptable to me. Each step I started to take from that moment on was from my Place of Power.

The same goes for the business example. I was able to show up the right way for the next launches because I visualized it beforehand. I knew that was the kind of business owner I would be if I was working from the Place of Power.

Journaling really helps with visualization too.

Here are a few questions you can answer during your journaling practice:

♦ How can I change my current perception to feel more in control?

♦ If I were in my Place of Power, what actions would I take?

♦ If I took those actions, how would I feel? What would I be thinking?

♦ What is the first step I can take right now to get into my Place of Power?

Step 3: Be Kind to Yourself [No Judgement Zone]

Throughout this entire process, you will be hyper-aware of how you think and how you have perceived previous instances in your life.

It can make you feel silly or weird or even ashamed for having those perceptions you must now unlearn. Remember to be kind and patient with yourself throughout the process. You can't hold it against yourself for the conclusions you drew back then. Those were probably formed as a way for you to cope with the incidents, and the subsequent actions were taken to the best of your abilities back then.

Accept the person you were back then. Accept that you were doing the best you could and that the person you are right now is still doing their best.

The important thing is that we recognize when we are acting from a Place of Insecurity and learn how to move away from it so that we can make decisions from a Place of Power.

The very act of recognizing that you are coming from a Place of Insecurity itself puts you in a Place of Power.

Lastly, there is no such thing as being completely insecurity-free. When you overcome a few insecurities, more insecurities will pop up. That's just how it is.

When you start your own business, it is unbelievable how many insecurities come up to the surface. Insecurities you didn't even know existed in the first place. At each growth stage, you will have a few insecurities that sabotage your business. It's hard work to overcome insecurities, no doubt, but the more you do it, the healthier decisions you can make for the growth of your business.

That's worth the effort, don't you think?

If you visit www.themarketingnomad.co/zero-to-four-figures, you'll get access to a printable workbook to implement this framework.

5.3

It's okay to take a breather.

It sounds silly even writing a lesson like this, but unfortunately, the toxic "hustle" culture in the entrepreneurial world has made this one of the most crucial lessons I've learned on this journey.

For those of you who may not be aware of the "hustle" culture, it's basically a notion that instigates and values workaholism, almost always at the expense of one's emotional, mental, and physical health.

I wasn't aware of how intense the hustle culture was until I stepped into the digital entrepreneurial world. Everywhere I saw, there was only one idea: if you weren't working, you were failing.

More importantly, if you weren't working, then everyone else around you was succeeding, and you would be left behind.

I have to admit that the hustle culture got to me. I stopped working because *I* wanted to work, and instead, I started working out of fear of being left behind. This transition from wanting to work to working out of fear was slow, and I didn't even realize the shift had happened.

It started with me refusing to take a break. I would work through the weekends and proudly talk about how it had been ages since I took a vacation. There would be days when I just wanted to rest, but I thought I needed to push myself to work through it because I believed that was the way to succeed.

Soon, I was starting to feel irritated about working. The minute I dreaded working at something I was passionate about, I realized something was wrong.

I was burned out.

I have talked about my massive burnout in the earlier chapters, and this was one of the reasons I contributed to it. It came to a point where I just did not want anything to do with my business, and I was seriously contemplating to quit.

I had reached a breaking point when I decided to take a two-month break. I no longer cared if I was behind. I no longer cared if other people were in front of me. I no longer cared about failing.

I just wanted to feel at peace again.

It was during this time that I started to question my thought process.

Did I have to wait for burnout to give myself permission to take a break?

Did I have to reach a breaking point to stop caring about where everyone else was on their journey?

Why did I feel guilty about taking a breather whenever I needed it?

I knew I shouldn't have had to wait for a meltdown or a massive burnout to signal that I needed to step back. There was something fundamentally wrong with that line of thought. I had found my passion after years of feeling lost, and for me to have felt so opposed to working was terrifying. I didn't want to force myself to do something I was passionate about.

As I recovered from my burnout, I felt my passion and desire to work return.

I decided not to quit the journey. Instead, I focused on how to sustain my passion and desire to work.

I've discussed this analogy on my social media pages and wish to share it with you. This analogy helped me break free from the toxic hustle culture, and I could move through my entrepreneurial journey in the way I wanted to.

Here's my analogy:

We're all in a race. You and I and everyone else.

But here's where everyone gets it wrong.

Each one of us has our own race, our own track, and our own finish line.

We've each got our own goals and our own path to take.

I've got my own goals and my own path to take.

You've got your own path to take. Your own goals to hit.

That means that you and I are participating in entirely different races.

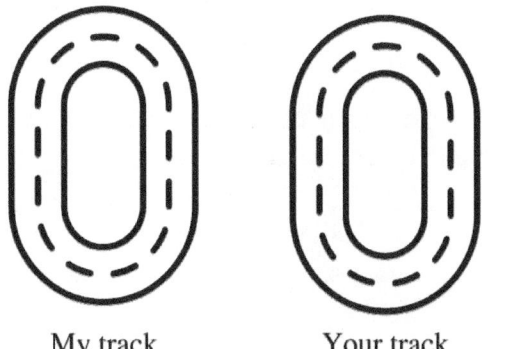

My track   Your track   Person X's track

Each one of us is running our own race.

It doesn't matter if you walk, jump, skip, run, crawl or even decide to take a couple of breaks in between; you will always win in the end because you are the *only one* running in your race.

The same goes for me. I've got my finish line to get to, and regardless of how I choose to get there, I will win because I'm the only one in my race.

The second I changed my perception, I no longer saw people running in my race; instead, I saw them running their own races.

I stopped feeling competitive. I stopped worrying if someone was going to get ahead of me or if I was falling behind.

I recognized the need to move at a pace comfortable for me and not anyone else. I didn't need to feel threatened or hurried to get to the finish line. In fact, I was actually happy for other people when I saw them heading to their own finish line, and this allowed me to cheer for them wholeheartedly.

By being the only one in my race, I was now happy. There were times I felt like running. There were times when I felt like I needed to rest. There were times when I felt like doing a slow jog. I did what I wanted to.

I stopped feeling pressured to work all the time. I started getting comfortable with taking a few days off from work. I became more aware of balancing my work and my personal life. I also consciously prioritized my emotional, mental, and physical health.

It's heartbreaking that I needed to have a massive burnout to recognize that it was okay to take a break, but I'm glad I learned this lesson.

When you recognize that it is okay to take a breather, it no longer matters to you how anyone else thinks your journey should go or how anyone else feels you should show up for your business.

You're on this entrepreneurial journey on your own terms, and really, there's nothing else that matters.

One of the reasons why most of us choose the entrepreneurial route is because even though it is hard, we want the freedom that comes with it.

If we rob ourselves of taking this journey on our own terms, aren't we refusing the very thing we are working so hard for?

5.4

Add self-care time on your work calendar.

After my burnout in June 2020, I knew I had to prioritize my self-care activities.

At this point, I had two different calendars. One was my work calendar on Google calendar, and another was my personal calendar in my personal journal. I listed out various activities. Calligraphy was one, nail art was another, and polymer clay craft was one more that I found interesting. I also wanted to make time to do a few puzzles.

I placed all of these activities in my personal journal. I gave myself an hour every other day to work on my chosen activity.

When I got back into full work mode after my two-month hiatus, it was hard for me to balance my work and personal life. I hadn't done a great job of it before and breaking some of my old habits was difficult.

I realized that I wasn't prioritizing my self-care because it was on another calendar. In my mind, I had to strictly follow my work calendar, but I felt kind of meh about my personal calendar.

I decided to transfer my self-care activities into my work calendar. Since it was on Google calendar, I blocked time off on the days I wanted to do self-care with yellow color.

I was reminded of my self-care time when I looked at my calendar to check for the next meeting. Given that I had this drive to complete everything on my work calendar, I started feeling weird if I wasn't checking "self-care" off my calendar.

Within two weeks, I became regular with my self-care activities.

It might seem odd to put something personal on a work calendar, and I giggle when I tell people about this move, but this turned out to be one of the best moves I made for myself and my mental health, which in turn, helped my business.

As entrepreneurs and business owners, we find it hard to turn our minds off when thinking about our business. There's always something to worry about. If things are not going well, we're thinking about how to fix it. If something is working well, we worry about how to sustain it. Prioritizing self-care doesn't come naturally to many of us, and it can be tough to pull yourself away from thinking about your business, which can contribute to burnout.

When you start putting your self-care activities on your work calendar, it's a way of telling yourself to intentionally break away from thinking about work. Having self-care as part of your routine is highly instrumental in maintaining your emotional well-being.

If you've struggled to prioritize your self-care, try this method out. We're wired to look at a work calendar and ensure we've completed everything, regardless of what is on there. So, when you put your self-care activities on it, you're immediately nudging yourself to do it, and you actually end up doing it.

Isn't that a massive win for you and your business?

5.5

Not every decision will be a smart one, and that's okay.

Growing up and even well into my early twenties, I never really cared about the decisions I had to take in life.

I always lived in the moment. I was your typical happy-go-lucky girl. I knew I could handle the consequences of my decisions, so I never paid much attention to them and went with the flow.

I always thought that the concept of making decisions was an irritating responsibility and a part of adulting that I couldn't be bothered with. That was until I became a business owner.

The minute I set up my company in August 2020, it was like a switch had flicked in my head. Suddenly, I became more aware of the decisions I was making for my business. There was this new feeling of caution with every step I was taking.

I had started the entrepreneurial journey a year earlier, in September 2019, but I was still pretty nonchalant about my decisions. Something about setting up my company made my mind feel that every decision I took from that moment on weighed significantly higher than any of the decisions I had ever made in my life. There was incredible pressure on me to get *every. decision. right.* It was a very unfamiliar and uncomfortable feeling for me.

I would think and overthink every decision, not wanting to mess up. I felt that every decision I made for my business had to be smart, or otherwise, I would be a failure.

I remember impulsively buying something for my company because a fellow entrepreneur had recommended it. I could barely afford it, and my bank account took a huge hit after that purchase. Turns out, the product wasn't intended for a business like mine. I hadn't done my complete research and had not considered the decision. I couldn't refund my purchase either. So that was a massive chunk of money that went down the drain.

That decision was not my smartest, and I was hard on myself for a long time. I rudely reminded myself that I was now a business owner and couldn't afford to make any foolish decisions. I kept basing my worth on this particular decision, even though plenty of other decisions I had made were right.

It really affected my mental health, and I got even more paranoid about each decision I was to make for my business.

Looking back, I don't think I should have been that hard on myself. Yes, of course, I learned from that mistake, and now, I wait at least 72 hours before moving forward with any purchase decision for my business.

Whether I learned something from it or not, I now know that putting that kind of pressure on myself was ridiculous.

As much as I want to be perfect, I am only human. Not every decision of mine will be a smart one, and that's okay.

It's easy to look at successful entrepreneurs or business owners and feel they always made the smartest decisions to get to where they are.

But the reality is a lot different.

We fail to realize that even with successful entrepreneurs or business owners, some of their decisions may not have been smart, which would have cost them in their journey.

But those decisions don't take away from the fact that they made many smart decisions that got them to where they are.

We're each on a unique path.

There isn't a roadmap to tell us how to make our decisions or which is the right way to go.

We're all figuring this out as we go.

None of us have this completely figured out.

That's one of the tricky things about the entrepreneurial journey too; just when you think you've got a good handle on it, something comes along and shifts you off-balance.

The entire entrepreneurial journey is a cycle of going off balance, learning to get back into balance at the stage of growth you're in, and then going off balance again, back, and so on and so forth.

So yes, naturally, sometimes you will slip up.

Yes, there will be consequences.

Yes, there will be lessons to be learned.

Yes, it will hurt.

Yes, it may take you some time to recover.

But that doesn't mean you should put insane pressure on yourself to get every decision right. That's a very unrealistic expectation and impossible to fulfill.

When you take the pressure off, you make better decisions because you base your decisions on clarity rather than fear.

You have to be kinder to yourself because regardless of how the consequences take shape, it doesn't take away from the decisions you have made right.

So, if you feel that insane pressure to get every decision right, and you will, I hope that this reminds you that sometimes you will slip up, and that's okay.

You may not have gotten it right this time, but that doesn't mean you will never get it right. It also doesn't take away from everything else you have done right, and it is not a reflection of your capabilities.

So, don't be too hard on yourself, okay?

5.6

Don't be closed off to the simplest route.

When I was studying in Singapore, the education system had a particular pattern.

When you reach fourth Grade, or as they call it, Primary 4, you take an exam at the end of the year that would streamline students according to their marks.

There were three streams: EM1, EM2, EM3.[8]

It was a highly competitive atmosphere because the streams determined your curriculum and the teachers assigned *(EM stands for English and Mother Tongue)*. EM1 stream was considered the crème de la crème. Every parent wanted their kid to get into the EM1 stream. There was a lot of pressure. *(Note: This structure no longer exists. The system changed right after I left Singapore.)*

Each of us was enrolled in tuition to help us prepare for this exam. I remember one mock exam where my tuition teacher gave us a few questions

---

[8] Auto, H. (2019, March 5). *From EM3 to subject-based banding: How streaming has changed over the years*. The Straits Times. https://www.straitstimes.com/singapore/education/from-em3-to-subject-based-banding-how-streaming-has-changed-over-the-years

to study beforehand. She told us that the questions appearing in her mock exam would be like the ones she had given us.

All I did the night before the exam was study those questions. Nothing else. I didn't revise any of her previous lessons. I felt pretty good about myself because I thought I had found a shortcut to getting good marks.

The next evening, I walked into my tuition class, feeling super confident about my preparation process. I sat on the first bench and waited for the mock examination paper. The paper was sealed, just like the actual exam, and when my tuition teacher told us to open our booklet, I broke open the seal excitedly and started to work on the questions.

I was able to do the multiple-choice questions with ease. As I came to the long answer questions, I realized that only two questions in the mock exam were from the list that was given the previous day. All the other long answer questions were not from the list. I panicked and did not remember any of the answers to the rest of the paper. Needless to say, I did not do well.

That was the day I learned two lessons:

1. Never trust the list of questions you're given before an exam.

2. Shortcuts don't work.

I think it's vital to explain what a shortcut is because that was a common misconception I had for many years.

A shortcut is a seemingly easy way to get to where you want to be, and it only seems easy because it usually involves skipping parts of the actual process to reach your final destination. Now because you've missed aspects of the process, the result is never what you wish for. Going through each part of the process is integral to getting you to the endpoint.

That's what people call an "easy route".

Now let me bring in a new concept. I'd like to call it the "simple route".

A simple route has all the steps in the process, and each of these steps has lesser complexity than the other routes that may exist to one's endpoint. So, we're not skipping any steps in the process, and we're still going to reach our destination, but only with the minimum effort required.

Over the years, I started to get a little confused. I did not understand the difference between an easy and simple route.

I started misinterpreting simple routes as shortcuts. I would be skeptical if a process seemed smooth and breezy. Even though the process was smooth-sailing, I would add unnecessarily complicated steps to feel I was not taking a shortcut.

I failed to realize that just because a process was simple didn't mean I was taking an easy way out.

I can't even begin to tell you the number of times I have over-complicated my life by overthinking the process.

A straight road from Point A to B would end up with me going all over the place and taking a longer time to reach Point B. Not only was it a waste of time, but it also drained my energy for no reason! I wasn't learning anything on this unnecessary detour, which only made the entire journey frustrating.

I kept doing this for a very long time, and I started getting miffed when someone would tell me not to take the "easy route".

After thinking deeply about this, I realized there was a difference between "an easy route" and "a simple route".

I started to look back at the times when the path was simple, but I refused to acknowledge it. Now let me be clear—the simple route doesn't mean it isn't difficult. It could be, depending on your destination.

A simple route is just the route that is the least complex of all.

Once I understood the meaning of a "simple route", I became more open to it. I was no longer unnecessarily complicating my life. I was going through all the steps and still learning the lessons. But the paths I now chose were always the least complex of all my options.

Let me give you an example.

When I started my Etsy shop, I intended to create a passive income source that could cover my monthly basic business expenses. With a passive income source like that, I knew it would allow me to focus my time on creating more passive income streams like content creation for my YouTube channel and Podcast, etc.

I also knew that it would allow me to choose consulting projects aligned with my interest since my basic business expenses would be taken care of by my passive income streams.

There were two different ways I could have gone about this.

One was to create a high-ticket product and sell at least three of those each month to hit my monthly goal.

In my opinion, the atmosphere on Etsy is highly competitive. Tons of sellers sell similar products, and one must stand out to succeed on Etsy.

For example, let's assume I was selling a high-ticket digital product on my website. I could sell the product at that price point for X amount of content. Given the high level of competition on Etsy, if you wish to stand out as a seller, one method would be to give buyers more value for their money. So if I wanted to sell the same high-ticket digital product on Etsy, I would have to include 3 x X the amount of content for the same price point.

Not just that, given that I was a brand-new seller, it would be harder for users to trust me. For users to be comfortable paying for a high-ticket product, I would need some backing from previous sales or reviews. I didn't have any of those at the time.

Even though this was a route to the endpoint I wanted, it was filled with many potholes.

My next option was to create multiple low-ticket digital products. I did the math. Given they were low-ticket digital products, I knew I could sell more of those each month. I calculated how many products to sell if I wanted to hit my monthly target.

This route was simple because I was a brand-new seller, and given the low price point of my products, I knew people would be willing to take a risk and buy from me.

Was this path a shortcut? No, it wasn't. I still had to take all the steps to make it to the end. But this path was simpler. There weren't any potholes, no unexpected detours, and no self-inflicted complications.

I took the second option. I slowly started adding more products to the mix. As I expected, my first sale came through. Then my first ten. Then my first fifty. As I added more products to the mix, I started seeing a monthly increase in sales. Soon, I was able to hit my monthly target very consistently.

It wasn't easy but *it was simple*, making all the difference.

In my business, and even in my recent personal life, I can give you so many more examples where I've consciously taken the simpler route. It has always led me to my destination with a sense of accomplishment and happiness.

I agree that shortcuts aren't the right way to go, but I also think it is essential for us to recognize which paths are just simple routes and which are actual shortcuts.

The next time you're faced with a decision about the path you should take, think about it for a second and ask yourself these questions.

- ◆ Is the path skipping the steps I need to make to get to where I want to be?

- ◆ Is the path filled with unnecessary detours and pointless actions?

♦ Am I adding unnecessary actions just to make it feel complicated?

♦ Is the path a simpler way to get to my destination?

♦ How can I simplify my path without skipping any steps?

When you take simple routes to get to where you want to be, you're allowing yourself to enjoy the process. I genuinely believe that's how every journey should be. You're not draining your energy unnecessarily, and you're focusing that energy where it needs to be—taking you to where you want to go.

There's a reason that more water and more electricity flows through the path of least resistance. *(Sorry, but the engineer part of me must equate it to this!)*

When there is least resistance, it does not mean that water or electricity is skipping steps to reach its endpoint. The path of least resistance isn't a shortcut. It's just the simplest way to get to Point B.

Water or electricity still moves through each path of resistance, but the path with the least resistance allows more current flow. More current, more energy.

I didn't make that up—that's Ohm's Law for you.

Don't be closed off to the simplest route; you'll be surprised how well you flow to your destination. And that's what we want, isn't it?

5.7

What are your non-negotiables?

I've always had a strong vision of the life I wanted to lead.

Yes, even as a kid, I just... *knew.*

During my engineering, things got complicated real fast for me.

Despite my strong vision, my decisions weren't aligned with it. In other words, I got lost and couldn't see a path toward my goals anymore.

When I left for New York in August 2016, I took it as a chance to reset my life. It was a way to regain control of leading the life I envisioned for myself.

At this point, I realized that I was too far from the path to my goals.

I didn't even know where to start and how I could get back to the kind of life I had envisioned for myself. It wasn't a game that I could just reset with the tap of the button.

As the engineer in me does with every single problem in my life, I decided to dissect the situation and come to its root.

It became clear that the core of my problem was that I wasn't making decisions aligned with the life I wanted to have.

For example, I envisioned a life where I was at peace with my surroundings. Yet, I was allowing the wrong people to stay in my life. There was still constant drama introduced by these people, and I didn't remove them from my life because I wasn't crystal clear on aligning decisions with my life's vision.

Thus, I built a framework that helped me make decisions in alignment with the life I envisioned for myself. This framework was very successful in my personal life, and when I became an entrepreneur, I decided to try this framework for my business decisions.

As entrepreneurs and business owners, we are plagued with many decisions.

Some of them are easy; some of them are hard. Sometimes, things can get so muddled that you're not clear about whether those decisions fit in the life you wish to have.

Whether the decision to be made is easy or hard, I've found that this framework of mine makes it simple to determine what decision I need to make to align my business with the life I have envisioned for myself.

I'd like to share that framework with you in this book in hopes that it would give you a good starting point to make decisions that are in alignment with the life you envision for yourself.

When I created this framework in 2017, I figured my three non-negotiables with these questions:

- ♦ What were 3 things that I absolutely needed in my life?

- ♦ What were 3 things that I would not settle for?

For me, it was **Peace of Mind | Happiness | Stability**

Now, it wasn't enough that I had these three non-negotiables. I needed to place conditions on my decisions to align them with my three non-negotiables.

So, the rules I placed for my non-negotiables were:

1. The decision is to be made in favor only if it adds to ALL three together.

This rule is as simple as it says. If I have to decide in favor, it must add to each non-negotiable I have, i.e., to my peace of mind, happiness, and stability.

Let me give you an example:

There's a friend in my life I'm happy talking to. There have been good conversations that add to my happiness bucket. But maybe this friend is just so critical most of the time that it borders on emotional abuse. When they behave this way, I can't feel peaceful around them. I'm always on high alert, bracing myself for their next brutal comment. They aren't adding to my Peace of Mind bucket at all.

That means they're not aligned with my life's vision, so I have to let them go. As painful as it may be in the moment, I cannot continue the friendship.

Without this rule, I would have continued being their friend and added constant drama into my life.

This rule ensures that every decision you make wholly contributes to your non-negotiables.

2. It's okay if the decision's outcome does nothing to the three.

Sometimes, we have to make neutral decisions. Decisions that will neither add nor subtract from any of the non-negotiable buckets. For example, the decision to make an acquaintance, or your everyday choices, etc., these do not add, nor do they subtract from your bucket, so it is okay to make a decision that is in favor.

3. If being in favor leads to an outcome that subtracts from any of them, the decision is a definite *NO*.

Sometimes, the outcome of a decision may add to one bucket but actively subtract from another. In this case, we have to choose not to move forward with the decision.

Let me give you a business example for this one.

When I had to decide whether to continue my membership program or not, I used this framework.

The membership program would have added to my Happiness bucket. I absolutely loved interacting with other business owners, which made me very happy.

Having the membership program would have added to my stability bucket too. The membership program had a monthly recurring revenue and a moderately predictable income. While the income wasn't sufficient to make financial sense for my business, it was consistent.

However, the membership program actively subtracted from my Peace of Mind bucket. I was juggling many things and couldn't give the membership program the time and effort it needed. Not just that, I knew that I would have more creative satisfaction with my Etsy shop, and I wanted to dedicate time to building that instead.

So, I made the tough call to end my membership program. I have no regrets. The decision I made at the time was in alignment with my life vision.

That's why I love this framework so much. When making decisions, I might not always consider how it affects my life long-term and whether it aligns with how I want my life to be. By having this framework, every decision, no matter how big or small, aligns with the life I envision for myself.

When I first started implementing this framework, it was a little tricky. I would write down my three non-negotiables on paper and put tiny boxes beside them. With every decision I wanted to make, I would draw arrows in the boxes to indicate if the decision was adding or subtracting to each of my buckets. I would put an up arrow if the decision added to my bucket and a down arrow if it was subtracting from my bucket. I would put a dash if it did neither.

This process now occurs on a subconscious level.

There are only three non-negotiables, which is all you must focus on.

There is no question of second-guessing your decisions either because you *know* that it is in alignment with your vision for life.

Yes, there are times when you will feel sad or angry or not at peace, but here's the difference: you've got a baseline set. Because of the framework, you will know how it feels to be in alignment with your life's vision. You know how you should be feeling. You know your endpoint. So, there is a definite direction you're moving towards even though, at the moment, you may not be in complete alignment.

In the last few years of applying this framework to every aspect of my life, I have never felt more aligned with my life's vision.

Now it's your turn. Let's start with this: What are your non-negotiables?

Visit www.themarketingnomad.co/zero-to-four-figures to get access to a printable workbook to get you started on your non-negotiables for a decision-making framework suited to your life's vision.

5.8

Stop focusing on the "Woman" in Woman Entrepreneur.

I've never considered myself a "Woman Entrepreneur".

Each time I was introduced as a "Woman Entrepreneur", it would tick me off. We don't call men who are entrepreneurs as "Man Entrepreneurs". That sounds ridiculous. We just call them "Entrepreneurs".

So why is there a need for an extra prefix for women?

I'll tell you why. It's a mindset problem.

When people think of the word "entrepreneur", the first image that comes to mind is a heterosexual cis man in a suit—probably posing on the front page of a business magazine. To make their mind accept women as entrepreneurs, people add something tangible to the word "entrepreneur". In this case, "woman" is added before the word.

Seeing the "woman" in front of "entrepreneur" makes people believe that an entrepreneur who is a woman is worthy of the title.

As women, it makes us feel confident that society will view us as an entrepreneur *because* the prefix exists. Without the prefix, we feel insecure because we don't fit society's image of entrepreneurs.

There's no distinction between masculine and feminine in the English language, so why do we feel the need to add something to an already existing word that perfectly describes exactly what we do or who we are?

You are an Entrepreneur. You are a Boss. You are a Hero. You are a CEO.

In case no one has told you this, you fully encompass the word in *all* your entirety—strengths, flaws, quirks, and all. You deserve the word. You do not need suffixes or prefixes to explain or prove why you deserve the word.

You. Are. Enough.

There have been many occasions where I've noticed people refuse to use the word "Entrepreneur" to describe me, but they were perfectly comfortable using "Woman Entrepreneur".

At first, I would go along with it, but I didn't like it.

Lately, I've started correcting them because I know I fully deserve the word "Entrepreneur". I don't care if they need any additional prefixes or suffixes to make *them* feel comfortable.

I also want to bring up the topic of equality. This book is written by an Indian, a woman, and an entrepreneur, so I'd be damned if we didn't bring up the concept of equality for women.

In this day and age, every person who identifies as a woman knows she wants equality. However, there is a false sense of security when we are invited to events specifically highlighting women.

Let me explain what's happened:

You feel you're on the front lines because of the focus on "woman". You see all these conferences for Woman Entrepreneurs or Woman in Tech. You feel you're now seated at the same table as everyone else.

That's actually not true.

You've been put at a separate table, but you feel recognized because you're the only category there.

In fact, you're willing to do anything to hang on to that table, even at the cost of your physical, mental, and emotional health.

Sometimes, you may recognize a huge disparity between the table you're at and the table you're supposed to be at, but you fear speaking up because you think you're being ungrateful. You can almost hear people say, *"Well, you wanted a seat, and you got it, so what's the problem?"*

You've been put at another table not because there aren't seats at the existing table but because people can't accept you being at a table that is perceived for another gender.

That's not what we want. That's not what equality is.

Equality is a seat at the ***same*** table.

That's where the difference lies.

We, as women, can't keep clinging to the table we've been given because we're afraid we won't be recognized at the actual table we're supposed to be at. A table for all genders.

Now that you've read this, you will see it everywhere around you. You'll see how women are placed in another category because society won't allow them to fit a word perceived for another gender.

Woman in Tech. Woman Business Owner. Woman Entrepreneur. She-CEO. And so on and so forth.

It will start to tick you off because you'll realize people can't accept you at the same table, but at the same time, they're pressured to give you a seat, so they give you a different table.

And we fall for that.

You aren't a "SHERO". You are a "HERO".

You aren't a "Woman Entrepreneur". You are an "Entrepreneur".

You aren't a "Woman Business Owner". You are a "Business Owner".

Own up to the table you belong to.

We can't demand equality when we don't believe we ARE equal.

Equality begins with us feeling confident that we will be recognized at the actual table we're supposed to be at.

Equality begins with us believing our seat is at the *same* table as any other gender.

Equality begins with you.

It begins with you believing you **ARE** equal.

You **ARE** worthy.

You **ARE** capable.

You **ARE** enough.

"I don't want a panel only for business owners who are women. Put me on a panel with all genders, and I am confident I will be enough."

That's the mindset we should be in.

I'll give you another reason why you should stop focusing so much on the "Woman" part of "Woman Entrepreneur".

In my journey as an entrepreneur, I've realized that facing the challenges unique to being a woman is more of a mindset shift than a strategy implementation.

As an entrepreneur who is a woman, I agree that there are unique challenges to this gender that will always be around. We have to work twice as hard to overcome some obstacles. There are also some obstacles that we cannot overcome, and we have to find ways to work around them.

However, each of us also faces other unique challenges regarding our race, religion, country of origin, work location, family upbringing, social strata, sexual orientation, gender identity, etc.

But does that make your journey harder?

You can't definitively say because every other person in the entrepreneurial world faces challenges unique to them. You can't compare, nor should you.

When you focus too much on the unique challenges of *one* factor contributing to who you are, you subconsciously implement the Baader-Meinhof phenomenon.[9]

The Baader-Meinhof phenomenon is when you're thinking of buying a red Volkswagen Polo, and you start seeing it everywhere on the road. It's the same concept here. When you focus too much on one factor that contributes to you as an entrepreneur, you start associating every problem you face as a result of that factor, whether accurate or not.

That's detrimental to your mental health, and it becomes easier to feel defeated at every step where you subconsciously associate every challenge with being a woman.

Being a woman should empower you, not demotivate you.

When you start to move away from the focus on "Woman" in "Woman Entrepreneur", you begin to feel that all the challenges you face are unique to you as a *person*. The challenges you face are not because of one factor that makes up who you are but a combination of *all* the factors that make up

---

[9] Kluchka, A. A. (2021). PSYCHOLOGY IN MARKETING: THE BAADER-MEINHOF PHENOMENON. ББК 65.42 С76, 12.

who you are.

Focus on your challenges as the result of all the unique factors that make you instead of focusing on the challenges that arise from one factor that contributes to you.

This way, you stop putting yourself in a box and find it much easier to overcome your challenges. Even if you can't overcome the challenges, this perception of your challenges will help you be open to finding ways to work around them.

You are an *entrepreneur*, so why not own up to it in its entirety?

CHAPTER 6
MONEY MINDSET

No money ☑

Little money ☑

More money ☑

Is it there or not; that is the question.

6.1

You have to unlearn your money mindset from your 9-to-5.

When I became an entrepreneur, I was aware that the fluctuations in my income would be drastic until I created enough systems to help me be more consistent with my income.

But it's very different knowing it and actually going through it. Even though I knew my income wouldn't be predictable, my behavioral patterns were still following someone who had a good, steady income. I dealt with money in the same mindset as I dealt with money at my 9-to-5.

When I started out, I was broke and did not know where my next month's income would come from. And yet, I was still holding on to the sense of security I felt when I had my full-time job. I just assumed the money would come the next month.

It sounds silly to even write it, but that's the reality of it.

For example, during the initial days, I bought loads of resources I thought I would need. Most of these resources had a monthly payment plan. When you have a consistent income with more or less consistent expenses, and you are thinking of hopping on a monthly payment plan, all you would do is calculate for one month. You can predict how long you can be on the monthly plan. That's the sense of security you get only with a consistent income.

It's different when you don't know how much you will be making the next month or if you will be making any money at all.

In my case, I was able to pay for the payment plans for the first month, and yes, maybe my savings were able to cover the second month. But the third month? I wasn't making enough yet to cover all of them. My continued sense of security from my full-time job had made me feel that money would come in and I would easily be able to pay it.

When I couldn't afford something as simple as a $12/month resource, I realized I had to unlearn many of my previous money mindsets. I needed to switch to a money mindset fit for the entrepreneurial journey.

My rational mind knew my bank balance was zero. I knew money was tight and that if I didn't book a client this month, I would be at a negative balance the next month. I knew I couldn't afford to buy more even though it worked out cheaper long-term. I had enough reasons to show myself how I needed to behave. But my money mindset was a reflex at this point.

Reason vs. Reflex, which one do you think had the upper hand? Of course, Reflex wins until you learn how to consciously choose Reason.

It's hard to recognize these reflexes, and it's even harder to unlearn them.

As someone privileged enough to be given a comfortable life by my parents, it was gut-wrenching to not be able to afford something as basic as $12/month. I felt so helpless. But I also recognized that things were different now, and I had to accept it.

I took baby steps.

In the meantime, I started to understand more about making money-related decisions as an entrepreneur. I factored the unpredictability of my income into my monetary decisions. I learned the difference between my 9-to-5 income and my current income. I began to incorporate new actions aligned with my current income flow. I consciously practiced each of those actions until they could overlap with my older reflexes.

Before starting this entrepreneurial journey, it is easy to feel you know what you're getting into. It's also easy to feel you are mentally prepared for it, and you'll act according to the situation.

It doesn't always happen that way, so here are a few questions to help you switch over your money mindset:

♦ Am I "spending money" or "investing" in the growth of my business?

♦ Am I basing my purchase decision on the income that has already come in or is yet to come?

♦ How much of my next month's income is predictable? Does this purchase fit within that portion of the income?

♦ If my entire income is unpredictable and I haven't budgeted it for this month, can this purchase wait till next month so I can base my purchase decision on money that has come in?

Understanding the difference between your previous full-time job to your current entrepreneurial job is just one part of a successful transition. You may think you *know* that things are different, but you don't always behave in alignment with them. You're used to thinking and responding familiarly. Some of those patterns are so imbibed in you that you don't even realize it.

The other part of a successful transition is unlearning the patterns that don't align and actively replacing them with patterns that align with where you are currently on your entrepreneurial journey.

The best way to work is to work from where you are, right?

6.2

Acknowledge your monetary limitations.

One of the most frustrating things about being a broke entrepreneur is, well, the *broke* part.

I can't even begin to tell you how many times I have yelled into my pillow about not being able to afford something for my business. It's a demotivating feeling and can really suck your energy. I had to learn this lesson pretty early on because it was affecting my mental health.

So first off, let me explain what was happening before I learned this lesson.

I would have this imperative need to buy whatever other businesses were using for their business. If I couldn't afford the resource *(which was ten out of ten times),* I felt that my business would never be as successful as theirs.

For example, if another solopreneur had hired an assistant to help them with tasks, I would think that they got their success because the solopreneur focused on CEO-related tasks only. In contrast, I had to focus on every aspect of my business. It left me bitter, and I did not like that feeling one bit.

I also found it hard to tell people that I could not afford something. I made some purchases even though I couldn't afford them because I wanted to "save face".

At any given point, I felt so restricted. I didn't have money to do what I wanted to do. I didn't have money to do what I needed to do. I hated being in that limbo.

Since I knew I shouldn't be making unnecessary purchases to prove a point and the bitter feeling was getting to me, I decided I needed to understand *why* I felt this way so I could move past it.

I knew I had monetary limitations. My bank balance always reminded me of that. But I realized I hadn't fully *acknowledged* and *accepted* my financial constraints.

In my mind, accepting I had monetary limitations made me feel like a failure, so I refused to do it. People would know my business was struggling if I admitted that I had monetary limitations. I was sure they would say I should have just taken a full-time job instead of starting my own business. I wasn't ready to handle their comments.

If I accepted that I had monetary limitations, then that would mean I had to change my behavior accordingly. I could no longer behave in the carefree way I did when I had a stable, comfortable full-time job. I was scared that if I accepted my monetary limitations, what felt like a temporary situation until now, would become a reality I had to face.

Would I be as happy as I was when I was carefree? Not knowing an answer to that was throwing me off balance.

I learned that it is not easy to accept where you are from a financial standpoint. We put so much pressure on ourselves because we perceive other people's financial situations to be much better than it actually is.

When you are an entrepreneur or a business owner, there's a lot of social pressure for your business to seem successful, regardless of the reality. People have this unrealistic expectation that if you're a business owner or an entrepreneur, you have to be successful because they feel there is no other explanation as to why someone would voluntarily put themselves through losses, debt, and financial restrictions to pursue the entrepreneurial route. It's hard not to succumb to that line of thinking.

During this time, I remembered my higher purpose, and this was one of the situations where it came to my rescue.

I wasn't doing it for the money. I was doing it because I was passionate about making a difference to the people around me. I genuinely wanted to help small businesses across the world to confidently implement their marketing strategies.

THAT was why I continued my entrepreneurial path.

If money wasn't my higher purpose for this journey, then why was I so concerned about what other people thought of me?

I could give two hoots to what people thought. If they thought I was broke, then so be it. After all, it was the truth.

If people thought my business wasn't successful, it was true that it was not financially successful *yet,* but I was making a difference. In my eyes, my business was successful in hitting its other goals. The money would take some time to come, but that didn't mean my company wasn't achieving what it was meant to do.

When this realization hit, I literally felt relief wash over me. There was no more proving anything to anyone. There was no need to fake anything, and I made more informed financial decisions for my business.

Just because this was my reality today did not mean it was a permanent situation.

If you'd like a starting point to acknowledging your monetary limitations, then here are some questions for you:

- ◆ Am I making this purchase decision because I have to or am pressured to?

◆ What is the maximum amount I can spend on a purchase without feeling stretched thin?

◆ Is the return on investment worth the purchase?

When you accept your monetary limitations, you change the game. You no longer purchase unnecessary resources because you feel pressured to. You will take your time to analyze what you need to buy, and you're more likely to make the purchase decision based on the return on investment for every cent. It will no longer matter to you whether people are judging you or not. People's perception of your entrepreneurial journey will be irrelevant, and you will start to appreciate the successes that you define for yourself.

You also understand what you can and cannot afford at the moment. This is one of the best skills that will help you regardless of the growth stage of your business.

You will also start to choose resources that fit your pocket instead of trying to expand your pocket to fit the resource.

I can give you an example: When I first started, I hired an independent contractor for four blog posts a month. I couldn't afford the four blog posts, but I kept justifying saying my business needed that frequency of blog posts to sustain. I don't remember where that came from, but I'm guessing that line of thought was inspired by a flourishing business posting four articles a month. I was expanding my pocket to fit the resource.

As I accepted my monetary limitations, it was clear to me that I could not afford four blog posts a month. So, I asked for two blog posts a month. That was a frequency I could afford, and it would continue to help my business. I adjusted the resource to fit my pocket instead.

Another good thing from acknowledging your monetary limitations is that you won't easily succumb to purchases made out of the Fear of Missing Out or what we marketers like to call FOMO.

It's easy to glance over your monetary limitations because you feel it is a temporary situation. But the longer you hold off on acknowledging what your monetary limitations are, the higher your chances of making your situation more permanent.

I will be honest, whether you acknowledge your monetary limitations now or delay accepting it, your ego will take a hit.

An ego hit now results from allowing yourself to control the situation. An ego hit later usually results from being unable to control or correct the problem.

Wouldn't you rather have the power to prevent a situation rather than lose the ability to fix it?

6.3

If there's money involved, it's not a hobby.

In June 2020, I realized that I had miscategorized my activities, which was one of the reasons contributing to my burnout.

Let me explain what I mean by that:

We all want a good work-life balance. It's easy to measure your work-life balance when working a 9-to-5 job. At a 9-to-5 job, you know when you're starting work and ending work. You can gauge when you're spending enough time on your personal life and you automatically know if the balance is off.

When you're an entrepreneur or a business owner, chances are, you are very, very, *very* passionate about what you are doing.

Because of that passion, you feel extremely happy when you're working. You feel like your soul is replenished. Time flies when you're deeply engrossed in what you're doing. I'm not saying that you can't be passionate about your 9-to-5 job, but when you're working on your own, there's a higher purpose to your actions, and working towards that higher purpose gives a different feeling.

You're building something from scratch and trying to make a difference in the world, and that feeling is unparalleled.

I counted on that feeling to keep me going.

I was happy in front of the camera, shooting YouTube videos or recording a podcast episode. Since I was happy doing these things, I thought I could slot them into the time I dedicated to my hobby.

I worked on other parts of my business throughout the day, and during the times I had set aside to work on my hobby, I would shoot a YouTube video, record my podcast episode, or even design content for my Instagram page. Given that these made me happy, I thought I was maintaining a good work-life balance.

Here's what happened after a few months:

Even though each of these activities made me happy, there was still a lot of time that went into strategizing them. There was pressure to build my audience, be it followers on Instagram, subscribers on YouTube, or even listeners on my podcast. Each activity was helping my business increase its revenue streams, and a lot was riding on every post, video, and episode.

Instead of working for a healthy amount of time every day, I was working through the time meant for my "me time". It's not surprising that I burned out.

I refused to acknowledge my burnout for a while because I had gotten into a routine. I was getting extra time to work on the other business-related activities.

If I kept that time only for my hobbies, how would I fit other business activities into my daily schedule?

I kept going and going until one day, I couldn't do it anymore.

While taking my two-month break, I recognized that I needed to categorize my activities properly. If there was money involved, then it was not a hobby.

It wasn't very simple to do that. I had to remove everything that reminded me of my business or was meant for my business. That included things like reading a business magazine or any kind of business book. Those were not hobbies and were meant to be read during my work hours.

It also meant that I had to decrease the frequency of my content to match the time I had planned for these business-related activities. After the burnout I had, I was ready to do anything to preserve my energy.

Once I recategorized my activities, I made sure I followed this one rule:

"If it makes me think about my business, it's not a hobby."

After a month of working on this new schedule, I felt much better. There was always tomorrow if I couldn't finish my work within my hours. I stopped being hard on myself. I allowed myself to feel content with the amount of work I had done within my work hours.

Over time, I could plan out my activities based on my work hours more accurately, and I continued to feel accomplished at the end of the day.

Also, during the time I had set aside for my hobbies, I only planned activities that refreshed and replenished my energy. My hobbies were now my feeble attempts at calligraphy, doing cute nail art, or even trying my hand at a 1000-piece puzzle. None of them made me think of work, and each activity gave me a breather.

As happy as they made me feel, my work-related activities were now restricted to my work hours only.

I still continue this even to this day. If it's a business book I'm reading or scrolling through Instagram to find inspiration for my next reel, I count it as part of my work hours.

Regardless of how passionate I am about my business, I recognize that I need time to let my mind rest and focus on other things that are equally important to me.

As an entrepreneur, I understand that our passion for what we do can make us feel like we can do it forever without burning out.

We fail to recognize that when there is money involved, it no longer is a hobby. When it isn't a hobby, all the stress of it being a business eventually catches up to you.

When you're thinking of doing something as a hobby, ask yourself these questions:

- ◆ Is it related to my business in any way?

- ◆ Does it make me think about my business or give me the space to relax?

If it helps you detach from your business, it's likely a good hobby to pursue.

Passion and burnout are not mutually exclusive, and we have to acknowledge that burnout happens to all of us if we don't take care. We must accept that work is work, and a hobby is a hobby. Wouldn't we all want a hobby that takes care of our mental health?

6.4

Plan out your multiple streams of income from the get-go.

In December 2019, I sat down to determine my income streams and realized this was going to take quite a bit of planning.

Some streams of income needed investments upfront, and others did not. All of them required a reasonable amount of time on my end to set it up. Given the varying amounts of investment for the income streams, I needed to plan my finances accordingly.

Remember, at this time, I could barely cover my basic business expenses with my freelancing, so I decided to go with the streams of income that did not need monetary investment upfront. These income streams, on the other hand, required a lot of time investment on my end to set them up.

One of my planned streams of income was my YouTube channel. Even as I'm writing this book, I am still giving my time investment to get my channel monetized. I get sponsorships and paid partnerships for my YouTube channel videos, which adds to my income stream. My YouTube channel also has my affiliate links, which adds to my source of income. But getting my YouTube channel to a point where it could add to my income took a lot of time and planning.

I planned for this book about two years ago. I knew this stream of income would need monetary investment on my end, and I had to make sure I reached a point where I could afford the investment to publish my book. There were expenses that I needed to save for. I would have eventually become an author, but I'm sure it would have taken me longer if I had not planned for it when I set up my company.

Here's how I planned my income streams:

Step 1: List out the possible income streams you'd like to have for your business.

Step 2: Determine when you would like to start putting the time to build the income stream.

Step 3: Approximately deduce how many resources you need for each income stream.

Step 4: Work backward *(as taught in Section 3.4)* and set up a timeline with actionable steps to acquire those resources.

Step 5: Revisit your plan periodically in case there are any changes. *(Example: More time to acquire resources, etc.)*

Fill the table below for each of your income streams.

INCOME STREAM:			
Resource & Steps	Timeline	From	To

Your table should look something like this:

INCOME STREAM: BOOK			
Resource & Steps	Timeline	From	To
$X for related costs	104 weeks	05/10/20	05/09/22
Step 1: Get 3 projects per month *(Set aside $y per job)*	104 weeks	05/10/20	05/09/22
Step 2: Save $z for unexpected costs	4 weeks	04/11/21	05/09/21
5,000 Email Subscribers	25 weeks	05/10/20	11/01/20
Step 1: Create lead magnet	1 week	05/10/20	05/17/20

When you plan your multiple income streams from the beginning, it gives you a head start. It may take a few months or even years for the income stream to be realized, but it gives you direction and helps you streamline your efforts if you put it on your radar. And doesn't streamlined effort maximize the return on investment for your resources?

Visit www.themarketingnomad.co/zero-to-four-figures to get access to a printable excel sheet to plan your income streams.

6.5

Passive income takes work.

When I started my entrepreneurial journey, I was fascinated with the concept of passive income.

From what I had heard from the people around me, passive income was income that was flowing in even when one wasn't actively working on it.

I imagined myself sitting idly on one of the many, many pristine beaches in Australia, sipping some fresh fruit juice as my bank account grew multiple folds, with absolutely no effort on my end.

Ah, that's the life I want for myself, I thought. So, I set to work to create as many passive income streams as one could possibly make for themselves.

When I started creating passive income streams for myself, it was clear that building them wasn't as easy as I thought it would be. I had heard a lot of misguided versions of passive income streams, and I felt silly to have fallen prey to that.

I decided to add this lesson to this book because my understanding of passive income is completely different now than my understanding back then. I had to learn the true meaning of passive income streams while working to create them.

I could say I felt a bit cheated by various people's declaration of their passive income, but on the other hand, I could have easily misunderstood as well.

The IRS defines passive income[10] as income you earn when you aren't actively or materially engaged. While that may be true from a definition point of view, the reality of sustaining a passive income involves active participation on your end.

When setting up my Etsy digital shop, I aimed to create a passive income stream for my business.

I put in a lot of work to create my first digital product for my Etsy shop. I made the product and posted it on Etsy in December 2020. Unfortunately, as much as I would have liked to book the next flight to Australia and watch the money pour in, my work did not end there.

I had to keep talking about my Etsy products on my other social media platforms. I needed to make sure that people finding me on other platforms were aware that I had an Etsy shop. I also had to respond to queries about my product and make sure I was helping potential buyers feel confident about my product. I also had to make sure the product was updated regularly.

I barely made six sales in the first two months of my Etsy digital shop. Just because I created a new passive income stream did not mean it gave me the income I desired from it right away. I needed to put in the time and effort to grow it, so I kept adding new products into the mix. This way, more people would find my shop. I also needed to keep working on the backend marketing, like the ads and the email marketing for my Etsy digital shop, to increase my products' visibility and, eventually, the sales.

My Etsy digital shop is a passive income stream for my business, and I don't deny it.

However, it may be helpful for me to mention *my* definition of passive

---

[10] *Publication 925 (2021), Passive Activity and At-Risk Rules | Internal Revenue Service.* (2001). Internal Revenue Service. https://www.irs.gov/publications/p925

income.

To me, passive income is when there is no correlation between the time you put in, to the income you earn.

The income I generate from a passive income stream is not dependent on the time I invest in the passive income stream. While I agree that my efforts to sustain my passive income stream are less than my effort to maintain an active income stream, I cannot deny that my passive income streams still require my consistent time and continuous attention to sustain them.

Many people brush off how much work actually goes into creating a passive income stream and sustaining it. It takes work to maintain and/or grow a passive income stream. You may not be actively working on it all the time, but that does not altogether remove the time and effort it needs. The word "passive" does not mean that you can let go after you create it.

Before you think about creating a new passive income stream for yourself, factor in that time and effort to sustain and/or grow it.

Better to know what you're getting into beforehand, eh?

6.6

Keep a separate "Business Savings" account.

I set up my company, The Marketing Nomad LLC, in Delaware, in the middle of the pandemic, a year after starting my entrepreneurial journey.

After setting up my company, I became a digital entrepreneur *and* a business owner. What I earned from that moment was no longer my "income" but my company's "revenue".

Until then, I always kept a certain percentage of my income as savings. My savings account was primarily there for me to fund my travels and vacations, but it was also an emergency fund.

When The Marketing Nomad LLC came into being, I thought having a checking account for my business would be enough. Having a savings account for my company didn't even occur to me.

Six months in, I hit an unexpected expense of about $400, and I had to use the money from my checking account. It was a big hit as I had other expenses for that month to take care of.

After that, I realized I needed to apply the same savings account concept to my business. I opened a business savings account. As I did with my income, I kept a certain percentage to transfer into my savings account each month.

Every month, after determining my business revenue, I would calculate how much needed to go into my business savings account and make the transfer.

Visit www.themarketingnomad.co/zero-to-four-figures to get access to a printable workbook to help you implement the below technique.

If you'd like to apply this for your business, here's a table to help you calculate the percentage going into your business savings account.

Step 1: Look at your monthly revenues in the past year. Pick the highest and the lowest revenue earned.

Step 2: Deduct all your expenses from the total revenue. Don't forget to include your pay, taxes, etc.!

Step 3: Calculate the remainder of your revenue.

Step 4: From the remainder, decide how much you would like to save. Choose an amount that you are comfortable with. You don't have to overextend yourself.

Step 5: Calculate the percentage of the savings with respect to the total revenue.

Complete the table below for the highest and the lowest revenue earned.

TITLE	$	%
Month Revenue		
Expenses		
Remainder		
Savings		

Step 6: Take the average percentage of savings in both cases. That would be a good starting point to calculate your savings each month. As your highest and lowest revenue changes with time, you can always repeat the process to find your new savings percentage.

For example:

TITLE	$	%
Highest Month Revenue	2,000	100
Expenses	1,100	55
Remainder	900	45
Savings	200	10

TITLE	$	%
Lowest Month Revenue	1,000	100
Expenses	800	80
Remainder	200	20
Savings	50	5

Average savings percentage = (10% + 5%)/2
                           = 7.5%

If your monthly revenue fluctuates too much, you might not be comfortable having a set percentage for savings. Even though the numerical value of 10% of 500 is lesser than 10% of 2,000, it's perceived a bigger hit. You may feel more comfortable having a lower percentage when your monthly revenue is on the lower end.

In this case, you don't need to take the average. You can keep it as a range *(In the example above, it would be 5-10% of the monthly revenue).* Your savings percentage will vary each month, depending on your monthly revenue. Contrary to popular belief, that is nothing to worry about. It is a natural part of the volatile stages of the digital entrepreneurial journey.

Your contribution to your business savings account may not be much for some months. But even a little going in each month will greatly help you in the long run. By factoring business savings into your list of expenses per month, you're allowing yourself to spread out paying for an unexpected expense in the future. If there is an unexpected expense, and trust me, that happens more often than you think, you'll have breathing space with your business savings account, and the blow is softer.

Backup plans >> no plans, am I right?

6.7

Know exactly how much revenue you are making each month.

When working full-time, I knew how much I made each month.

I would get an email from the accounts department with my bi-weekly pay stub details. I would enter my password and look at the pdf to see how much money would be credited into my bank account. There was only one source of income, and the emails from the accounts department helped me track my money.

When I started as an entrepreneur in September 2019, I only had one income stream, and it was easy to track how much I was earning.

After setting up my company, The Marketing Nomad LLC, in August 2020, I added more income streams.

As I write this book in 2022, my company has five income streams, four of which are passive and one active. Once I release this book, it will add to another stream of passive income for my company.

One of the things that I've realized as a digital entrepreneur and business owner is that it is harder to track your total income per month when money is coming in from different streams.

When it gets harder to track, it gets harder to know where your business stands. It also becomes challenging to make decisions because you don't have complete information about what income your company has made that month.

In the first few months that I had multiple income streams, I knew exactly how much money was coming from each of the individual platforms. You could wake me up in my sleep, and I'd tell you how many sales I had made or what my revenue generated from a specific income stream was. But if you asked me how much I was earning each month in total, I would draw a blank.

That was a behavioral pattern that I was carrying forward from my 9-to-5. You see, at my 9-to-5, I only had to register the pay stub amounts in my mind. That was it. My total income for the previous two weeks was written on the pay stub. That was enough information for me to calculate what I could afford and what I couldn't afford. When it came to my business, knowing how much I was making on each income stream was important, but it wasn't sufficient to help me analyze what my business could and couldn't afford.

At one point, I hired an independent contractor based on information I had from knowing how much I was earning from individual income streams. Within a month, it became clear that I couldn't afford to continue with the independent contractor. If I had summed up my income streams and known how much my company was making, I would not have moved forward with this decision.

It was a really tough conversation with the independent contractor that I couldn't move forward with them. They were very excited to take on my project, and their enthusiasm was infectious. I, too, was excited to work with them to revamp parts of my business. I was disappointed when I realized I had made a mistake. Even though they were very understanding, I knew I could have avoided the entire situation if I had just been a little more aware.

That made me feel worse. I knew I had to start consolidating my income streams every month and be more responsible as a business owner.

It sounds simple when you read it. You may ask me how difficult it is to determine how much income your business makes per month.

I'm not saying it is difficult, but I am saying that it is a new behavioral pattern you have to unlearn and learn again to match your current needs.

Here's how you can get into the habit of tracking your income streams:

Step 1: Open an excel sheet and list all your income streams.

Step 2: Add a column for the total revenue, transaction fees, miscellaneous charges, and gross profit.
(Pro tip: The simpler it is, the more likely you will do it regularly)

Step 3: Fix a day each month to work on your KPI[11]. I like to call this KPI Day.
(For example, my KPI day is the first Saturday of every month. On the first Sunday of every quarter, I have another KPI day to look over the previous quarter and determine strategies based on my conclusions.)

Step 4: Add this to your calendar so you will be alerted.
(Pro tip: It helps not to keep other tasks on KPI day, so you're not pressured to hurry. This also gives you time to reflect on the previous month's stats and strategize your next steps.)

When you have only one source of income, your pay stub notifications or your bank account notifications will give you the necessary information. When you have multiple sources of income, you get notified of each income stream. Unless you're a mental math genius *(as much as I love math, I'm not)*, you can't figure out how much you're making in total just by the individual notifications. Isn't it better to leave it to excel to track it for you?

---

[11] KPI: Key Performance Indicator

CHAPTER 7
RELATIONSHIPS

Family ✔

Friends ✔

Peers ✔

They're as important as your business.

7.1

It takes a village to grow your business. Choose your village wisely.

I remember calling my mom from Long Island in June 2019 to tell her I was starting on my own.

Without hesitation, she asked, *"Okay, what do you need?"*

The same continued for everything I told her from that moment on.

"Ma, I think I will start a YouTube channel."
"Okay, what do you need?"

"Ma, I'll also do a podcast?"
"Okay, what do you need?"

"Ma, I think I should set up my company in the US."
"Okay, what do you need?"

"Ma, I'll do a shop on Etsy too?"
"Okay, what do you need?"

You have no idea how relieved I would feel each time she asked that question with no hesitation. To me, it felt like she trusted my decisions. Her immediate response always made me think that she believed in my potential.

When I'm recording a podcast episode or a YouTube video, she goes, *"Shhhh, she's recording!"* to everyone in the family. When I'm stressed out, she sits down with me and talks me through my thought process. She makes sure I eat on time. She gives me fruit every single day. She encourages me to be healthy. She reminds me to stay humble. Anything I need, all I have to do is ask her, and she will move heaven and earth to make it happen.

On this journey, I have lost faith in my potential several times. But knowing that she firmly believes in my potential has always brought back my belief in myself.

My dad always makes time for me when something is bothering me at work. He may have a million things to do, but all I have to say is, "Papa, I'm not getting this," and that's it; he is there for me. He walks me through what I'm struggling with and helps me see things clearly. Knowing he is there for me takes the weight off my shoulders.

My sister, Pinky, is always there when I need a second opinion. She's my biggest cheerleader. Especially when I fail to see, she reminds me of what I can accomplish. Her unwavering faith in me surprises me and has pulled me out of some very dark places over the years.

People think that as entrepreneurs, all we need is financial support. I don't think that way at all. I believe emotional support is most important. The people you surround yourself with may or may not be able to understand what you do, but having their support makes you feel invincible.

I do agree that I am fortunate to have such strong family support. I know it is a privilege that I must never take for granted. I also do acknowledge that not everyone will have the same kind of support from their family as I have.

For that, I want to say that your village consists of people you can lean on. They don't have to be related to you but must be supportive of your journey.

I can say that my close friends have helped me on this journey in so many different ways. I have friends who have been a part of my life for a while; I also have made friends along this journey, and I can say with utmost confidence that their support has given me a lot of courage to keep going.

I remember calling up one of my best friends in the middle of the night, crying because I couldn't see a path forward. This was during the period of lull in my business. She calmed me down first. We sat on the call, each of us with our laptops out, and we began researching my next possible steps. Just knowing that there is someone out there who really cares about me and is willing to spend time with me to figure things out was such a precious feeling.

When you start on your own, it's not the same as working a 9-to-5. Everything is on you. A lot is riding on the risks you've taken to start and grow your business. There's also a lot of pressure and stress with the territory. Not just that, there will always be imposter syndrome lurking in the corner and a ton of self-doubt ready to attack you at a moment's notice.

Yes, I agree that part of this journey is about learning how to cope with that by yourself. I don't deny that I have had to do a lot of work to ensure that my mental health is in a good place. But when you have the right people around you, it just makes everything a lot lighter.

It takes a village to grow a business. If you think you can do it alone, I guarantee you cannot.

I think that we hear the term "self-made", and we make ourselves believe that we don't need anyone else's help. But every "self-made" person has taken help and support from the people around them. It might not be "support" in the traditional sense of money, but there are other kinds of support too.

Be it one partner picking the kids up from school because the other partner had a client meeting. Or that one aunt who always likes your posts for your business, even though they have no clue what your post is about. Or even a client of yours talking about you with their friends and spreading the word about you. Or a particular follower who always comments on every story you post. Or your entrepreneur friend who checks in with you every now and then, just to see if you're okay.

There is no one way to support, and we as entrepreneurs need to recognize this. You need people on this journey who will be by your side.

Along this journey, you will find people who want to be a part of your life only to drain your energy. You will also have people who unintentionally do it too.

One of the most painful things you will have to do on this journey is recognize who cannot come along with you.

You can choose who you want in your life.

You get to choose your village.

And you get to choose your village *without feeling any guilt.*

That is not being selfish. It is an act of self-love to ensure that you choose the right people to come along on this journey with you.

If you know that the people you choose will impact your journey, wouldn't you want to take the time to choose wisely?

7.2

Build relationships first; worry about stats second.

Because of my instincts as a marketer, I focus a lot on stats.

When you are a marketer working at a company, relationship building is usually between the customers/clients and the company as a whole. You strategize marketing campaigns so that people feel more connected to the brand and help them recognize that the company cares about their needs.

So, when I started this journey, I couldn't shake off the marketer in me. I continued my same focus on stats. I was figuring out strategies for people to feel more connected to my brand and for people to know that my company valued them.

What I didn't consider was that I was building a personal brand. *I* was the face of my company. My company was a vague entity to them. More than my company valuing them, my customers/clients/followers/subscribers /listeners needed to know that *I* valued them.

As much as I had a company backing me, I had to use unique strategies for my personal brand.

For example, as a marketer at a small business, my job would be to ensure that customer service was on point for the audience. There would be messages on social media platforms with questions by potential customers about the products. I would answer them promptly, or they would request more details about the product/service, and I would ensure they got all the information they needed. The interactions with the audience were pretty straightforward.

As a business owner who was now the face of her company, the interactions with my audience weren't so straightforward anymore. My audience wanted to get to know me. They needed to understand me so that they could trust me. They wanted to feel comfortable before recommending me, be it my social media pages or my products/services.

But here I was, not realizing that I was now a business owner, and not just a marketer. During the initial few months of this journey, I only interacted with my audience as a marketer. My conversations with them were solely focused on increasing my stats in some way. The conversations were about getting them to follow me, share my content, recommend my page, or opt for my products/services.

Of course, that backfired massively.

I didn't understand that since I was the face of my brand, forming a relationship with me was my audience's way of doing their research. For brands with no personal branding involved, the audience would check out their website and social media accounts, look at testimonials, understand the brand's vision, mission, etc., build their trust, and then decide to purchase from the brand. While my audience did all of those things with my brand, there was one more factor they wanted to include in their research—*Me*.

So, when they reached out to me in my direct messages on social media platforms, they weren't ready to buy my product/services or recommend my pages to anyone. They wanted to build a relationship with me first. They wanted to have a no-pressure conversation with me.

I thought of myself as a marketer and started talking about my products/services. They weren't interested in my products/services just yet, so I ticked them off because I kept shifting the conversation to my products/services.

Within two or three conversations with the people in my direct messages, I could gauge that something was amiss. They would disappear the minute I started talking about my products/services, which to me, as a marketer, was clear that they weren't nurtured enough.

After pondering a little more about what was amiss in my own marketing for my personal brand, I realized I had overlooked myself as part of the nurturing process for potential clients/customers. After all, I was building a personal brand and needed to include myself in the nurturing process.

I shifted my focus from showing up as a marketer and decided to show up as a business owner who was building her personal brand.

Instead of intentionally steering all the conversations toward my products/services, I became genuinely invested in building relationships with my potential clients/customers first. The discussions in my direct messages were more casual, and I allowed the conversations to flow the way my potential clients/customers wanted to, as long as it was within my healthy boundaries.

It took a few months for people to warm up to me and fully trust what I could help them with. It also took a lot of back-and-forth conversations between my potential clients/customers for them to feel ready to opt for my products/services. During this time, I had around four or five launches. From the results of the product launches, it was clear that they were still not yet ready. There were a few inquiries for my last few product launches but little to no conversions into sales. I still kept going. I continued my focus on building relationships instead of focusing on my stats.

Finally, for my seventh product launch, I had forty people sign up within a week, and 90% of them were people I had been having great conversations with over the past few months. Throughout those conversations, as much as I had hoped that someday I could help them with my products/services, I just focused on getting to know them and allowing them to get to know me. I continue this even to this day. I focus on building relationships with my audience first.

Whether you are a digital entrepreneur building your personal or business brand, you are a part of the marketing. You are in the equation. You are one of the most important factors people will consider when purchasing your products/services, so allow your followers/subscribers/potential clients to get to know you.

A few ways you can go about this are:

♦ Share content about yourself, your mission, and your values. What is your work ethic like? What is your thought process like? What is your ultimate goal? What does a day in your life look like?

♦ Share content about your thoughts on recent events or industry news.

♦ Show off your personality! If you've got a quirky sense of humor, let people see it. If you're meticulous, show people your checklists and productivity hacks. Let them get a sneak peek of who you are as a person.

♦ When interacting with your followers/subscribers, ask them what kind of content they would like from you. Focus on fulfilling their needs first. Talk to them like you would talk to a friend.

Over time, you'll be surprised that the biggest reason people have chosen your products/services is because they value *you.*

I know that it can seem a bit odd when you find yourself part of the marketing equation, but when you focus on building relationships as a business owner, it becomes easier for you to allow people to add you as part of their research.

After all, you are the biggest strength of your business. Why not allow people to factor that into their purchasing decisions?

7.3

It's okay to ask for help or lean on trusted people for support.

As a kid, I had two things that always appeared on my report cards.

Different year, different teacher, but consistently the same report card comments.

One, that I was independent, and two, that I was very talkative.

I took pride in both, even though I don't think their description of me as talkative was meant as a compliment.

I loved being called independent and liked making my own decisions. I knew what I wanted and what I didn't like. I enjoyed doing things on my own.

I grew into my teens, and I continued to be independent.

I was confident, and I liked taking risks. I knew who I was, and I liked the autonomy.

I'd often hear people say, *"Oh, Prithvi? She doesn't need help from anyone,"* or *"Prit's so independent. She'll do it by herself."*

Oh, how I beamed whenever I heard people say these things about me.

As I got into my twenties, life got a bit harder.

I was no longer building blocks; I was trying to build my life.

I was no longer playing with toys; I was toying with career options that I wasn't happy with.

I was no longer losing games during Physical Education class; I was losing sight of myself.

I was no longer placing pieces of a puzzle together; I was trying hard to piece my broken heart together.

But I was independent, right? How could I ask for anyone's help? What would people think if I asked for help? I was the girl who did everything on her own, and if *I* asked for help, then wouldn't people think less of me?

I don't know how it happened, but somewhere along the way, I mistook being independent as not asking for anyone's help. I thought being independent meant doing everything by myself. I couldn't bring myself to break the image that people had of me right since my childhood.

I remember the time I had to move from Rochester to Long Island.

I had just gotten my first full-time job and had to pack everything in my home. I refused to ask anyone for help. I packed my stuff into twenty U-Haul medium boxes. Twenty boxes because I only packed them to the amount of weight I could carry. It would have been much less than twenty boxes if only I had asked for help, but I didn't want anyone thinking less of me.

I carried all the boxes into the U-Haul truck that I had rented. It took me a long time to do it. Again, I did not want to seem weak or let anyone think I wasn't independent.

What an unnecessary mistake that was. I ended up with a whole-body cramp, and I couldn't move for the next two days. My job was starting on Monday, and here I was, on Saturday, unable to move any part of my body without significant pain.

When my visa didn't process, I was so deep in the hole that I didn't care what anyone thought of me.

I couldn't do it on my own. I just couldn't. I barely had the will to see the next day. Living up to my image of being independent was the farthest thing from my mind.

I asked for help each time I needed it. I needed help selling my car and asked my colleagues for help. They went above and beyond for me, asking all their contacts. I cried when one of my colleagues told me someone they knew was interested because that feeling of being helped was so foreign to me. Each one of my colleagues helped me in every way they could. They also gave me words of encouragement when I needed it the most, and I will always be grateful to them.

I needed help packing my things, and I asked for help. Three of my colleagues/friends came over the weekend and looked ready for war. They helped me pack my stuff and cleared my entire house with me. My mattress was really heavy, and only two of us were around at this point. We couldn't carry it to my friend's truck, so we ended up rolling it on the street, which was hilarious. My friends/colleagues made every minute of my last few days on Long Island fun. One of them even saw me off at JFK International Airport, which meant the world to me.

My mom's elder brother in Philadelphia called me every day for the two weeks leading to my flight back to India. He wanted to be there for me in any way he could and knowing that I could lean on him for support added a layer of relief that I wasn't used to.

When I was at the Abu Dhabi airport during my layover, I cried so much that I was scaring the people around me. I knew I couldn't keep doing that, so I asked my friends to calm me down. They immediately called me, and we spoke till I calmed down. It really touched my heart.

Even to this day, those twenty-four hours of my journey back to Bangalore are an absolute blur.

I don't remember sitting in either of the two planes or anything else about my journey. I only remember sitting at the far end of the rows of empty seats at Abu Dhabi International Airport, crying into my phone and allowing myself to be consoled by people who cared about me.

My mentor checked in every day after I landed to ensure I was okay. I asked him for help with my website and the project I had just gotten. He was always there by my side, every step along the way *(and continues to do so, too!)*.

None of them thought any less of me.

The people in my life still knew I was independent.

They still thought I was badass.

They still believed in everything that I was capable of doing.

To each one of them, I was exactly the same person I was before I asked for help.

That was such a powerful realization for me. From that moment on, I changed my definition of being independent and learned it was okay to ask for help.

Our drive to be independent is one of our inherent traits as entrepreneurs. Especially on this journey, there is so much pressure to have it all together or to seem like you have it all together.

It is not easy asking for help, and no one knows this better than I do.

But being independent does not mean you cannot ask for help.

Being independent means that you recognize the situations when you need help and you ask for it.

It also means allowing yourself to lean on your trusted people for support.

With the ones who really care about you and want to be there for you, all you have to do is ask. You'll never feel like you are a burden with the right people. The right people will never think less of you for asking for help.

Remember, no one said you had to be alone on this journey, nor do you have to do everything yourself.

If you need help, it's okay to ask. If you need support, it's okay to ask.

Isn't that a more straightforward way to go about this journey?

Your friends and family may or may not be able to help you. Don't hold it against them.

During my engineering days, I wasn't making the best decisions.

There was a lot of self-inflicted drama in my life, and I was in trouble most of the time. I had some help from my friends and family to escape a few sticky situations. For other problems I found myself in, they couldn't help me out even though they wished to. For those situations, I had to work things out independently and figure out ways to overcome the mess I was in.

I learned a critical lesson then. As much as my friends and family cared about me, that didn't mean they could always help me. Sometimes, external circumstances were preventing them from helping, or they had their own problems to work through. Either way, I knew I couldn't hold it against them, and I always appreciated it whenever they could help me.

When I started my entrepreneurial journey, I assumed each one of my friends and extended family would tell all their networks about my marketing services. Some did recommend me, and I was grateful.

However, some of the people I thought were a sure shot to recommend me did not. That hurt a bit. I reasoned that I would have done that for them if they had started something on their own. Even though I had learned from my engineering days that sometimes my close ones won't be able to help me out, I failed to apply the lesson here.

Of course, when you're building a business from the ground up, you are emotionally invested in it. When emotionally invested, it is easy to have unrealistic expectations and take other people's actions personally.

As I struggled to get each client for my business, I wondered if they weren't recommending me because they didn't trust my potential or that they wanted to see how I would manage it on my own. With all these thoughts circling in my head, I felt very resentful.

Over time, during random conversations with them, I understood some of the real reasons why they weren't recommending me. One was that they didn't know anyone looking for my services. Another reason was that they didn't completely understand what I was doing or how I could help businesses. Another was that they had a lot going on in their lives and were entirely focused on that.

All these reasons seemed perfectly valid, and I'll admit, I felt a bit ashamed for being resentful. While there were one or two people who didn't recommend me for the reasons I thought, it was unfair of me to assume everyone had the same thought process.

It took me some time to realize that my resentment came from my insecurities. I felt the need to rely on other people's recommendations because I did not trust myself to bring in clients with my own efforts.

As entrepreneurs, we must recognize that the responsibility of growing our business is on our shoulders.

If anyone is helping us, that should only *add* to an existing stable foundation that we have built for ourselves. It shouldn't be something we rely on. You can't hold it against them because no one is obligated to help you.

To be honest, the only person who owes you anything is you.

No one else.

Now, I agree that there will be people who don't want to help you because of jealousy or their need to see you fail.

As you trust yourself more, you also stop holding it against them. You recognize that they are coming from a Place of Insecurity, and it is not your job to fix it for them. Either case, you're allowing yourself to be in the healthiest mindset, right?

CHAPTER 8
LOSSES & WINS

Hiccups ✓

More hiccups ✓

Eventual successes ✓

Success isn't the end point.

8. 1

Just because something in your business was not successful, does not mean that you are a failure.

When I had to shut down my membership program, it meant the product had failed.

I found it hard not to take it personally. For some reason, I felt that sustaining my membership program was a testament to my intelligence and my abilities. If I was intelligent enough, then I would have been able to sustain it, I thought. The closer I came to the decision of closing the membership program, the deeper I dug myself into a hole.

Around that time, my business had also been in a lull for a few months. My business was crumbling around me, and I was beginning to feel a similar loss of control that I felt exactly two years ago when my visa did not get processed.

Here's what we all need to remember: Healing is not linear. You think you might be over it, and you've healed completely. But you find yourself in a similar situation, and once again, you spin right back to where you started.

That's what happened to me too. The more I couldn't control what was happening to my business, the more I remembered how I felt when I couldn't control my visa not being processed. I thought I had worked through all those feelings, and yet, here they were, coming back to me again.

It was pretty messed up.

What was infuriating for me was that I had *just* worked through all of these feelings.

I *just* gotten over feeling all those horrible things.

I was *just* beginning to feel lighter about where I was, and to feel despair all over again; I could feel my strength breaking bit by bit, day by day.

My anxiety started rising again. I could feel myself panicking in the middle of the day. I felt the same dread creeping over me as I thought about possibly closing down my business. I could almost hear what everyone was going to say; that I couldn't even sustain my entrepreneurial journey for two years. I felt like I was letting down everyone who believed in me.

Yes, healing isn't linear. But here's one more thing that I didn't realize at the time. This time around, I was better equipped to handle my emotions. I had learned how to get out of feeling despair, and that knowledge wasn't going anywhere. When it came to handling the adversity, I wasn't starting at ground zero. It may have felt like I was back in the same place two years ago, but I wasn't. It was just a dip along the way, and if I could figure out how to rise from ground zero, I sure would know how to rise from this dip.

As I started to recognize that I wasn't in the same place and that it was just a dip, I felt a little bit stronger. I started implementing everything I did when I felt this way the last time around.

I knew what worked. I started with those. I increased the frequency of my meditations. I started journaling three to four times a day.

Each time I felt a different feeling, I'd write it down. I wouldn't judge myself for any of my feelings. Writing it down was just a way for me to unravel the thoughts in my mind.

When I started writing my thoughts down, I recognized what was working with my business and what wasn't.

Yes, I was in the middle of a pandemic, and naturally, my business was taking a hit, but there were also other areas that my business was lacking. These were systems and processes that I needed to fix or align better. The fact that I could recognize what was going wrong was a huge indicator that I was capable, and this had nothing to do with my potential.

My business' status was a culmination of both internal and external factors. It did not mean I was a failure. It just meant I needed to focus on the factors I could control. And so I did.

Over the next few months, I could see a remarkable improvement in the backend processes and systems for my business. Things started looking up for my business. It wasn't only because I worked on the factors I could control. I was lucky that the factors outside my control also shifted and became more favorable for my business. It was a combination that led to things turning around for my business.

Even if it did not, and I had to close down my business, I would have been sad, but I also would have recognized that it did not mean I was a failure.

There are a lot of factors that go into whether a business is successful or not. The same goes for your products or services. Some factors are in your control. Some are not in your control. Some factors you have the time to mitigate. Some factors you just have to play ear by ear.

In any case, as much as you feel responsible for your business, you can't take it personally. Your contribution to the business is just *one* of the factors affecting it. What's on you is working your best on the factors you can control which also means you are giving yourself the best chances for success, doesn't it?

8.2

The 6 Month Rule.

In the beginning few months of 2021, my business was at a standstill.

We were fast approaching the first anniversary of the World Health Organization declaring COVID-19 a pandemic[12], and businesses weren't sure if they would even exist a few months from then. Investing in a marketing strategy consultant was the last thing on their minds.

I wasn't sure how long I could sustain myself as a business owner as it had been a few months since I last booked a client. I was seriously debating if I should quit the journey and get a full-time job. Not that getting a full-time job in the middle of a pandemic would be easy, but I thought maybe this was the end of my entrepreneurial journey.

I remembered another time I wanted to quit.

When I was six, my mom wanted me to join Bharatanatyam classes. I was already doing Bollywood performances on stage. Given that I self-taught Bollywood dancing, my mom felt it was her responsibility to help me hone my natural talent.

---

[12] Cucinotta, D., & Vanelli, M. (2020). WHO Declares COVID-19 a Pandemic. *Acta bio-medica : Atenei Parmensis, 91*(1), 157–160. https://doi.org/10.23750/abm.v91i1.9397

I did not want to enroll in Bharatanatyam classes at all. I just wanted to keep doing Bollywood dancing. Also, I was not a fan of structured classes from a very young age. I liked to do things on my own and at my own pace. I didn't like people telling me what to do. I was very stubborn *(still am, though now, life has smoothened my rough edges a bit)*.

I remember my mom telling me that I should at least try it for six months. If I didn't like it, I could quit. She said that I had to be neutral during the six months. I had to give it my all and make a fair decision at the end of six months. She hoped I would change my mind once I learned the dance form.

I went to every weekly class for six months. A few times, I cried before going to class because I just did not want to, but I diligently went. I practiced the hand movements at home; I did the homework my teacher would give. My mom said six months, and I held her to her promise.

After six months, I still felt the same, so I quit.

What stayed with me was the concept of six months:

Give it your all for six months; if you still feel the same, you can decide.

Even without my knowledge, I have applied this concept throughout my life. I never thought it to be a "6 Month Rule" explicitly, but if I look back today, there was a pattern of me trying something for six months and then deciding.

It's absolutely crazy how something from one's childhood can have such a profound effect on one's adulthood. Well, maybe not crazy because that's probably the basis of every therapy session.

I decided to use the 6 Month Rule for my business. I would give it my all for six months without expecting anything, and if I still felt the same after six months, I would quit.

When you apply the 6 Month Rule, you have to make sure you are giving it your all during the six months. If you pause in between, the clock resets. I didn't make this rule; my mom did. Honestly, I think she hoped the clock would keep resetting and I would go to the Bharatnatyam classes forever. Turns out, what she didn't count on was the fact that I was *her* daughter, and I was just as headstrong as she was.

Back to my current situation, I gave it my all for six months without expecting anything in return. I added more lead magnets. I revamped the sales funnel to make it more segmented. I changed the content for my social media pages. I made my entire backend marketing more efficient.

Instead of worrying about getting a client, I used this time to fix the backend processes of my business. I set up new systems so my life as a business owner would become easier.

Maybe because I was no longer worrying, I could see things more clearly. I was able to see what was going wrong and what needed to be fixed. I also figured out ways to sustain what was going right.

I continued adding products to my Etsy digital shop. I improved the backend processes for my Etsy digital shop as well. I also spent time learning more about marketing and business and improving my knowledge.

Within three months, everything looked different on the backend. I was more confident about my business by the sixth month, even though I didn't get any clients. I knew the processes and the systems were going to work. It was only a matter of time. I decided not to quit and to keep going.

Towards the end of the seventh month and the beginning of the eighth month, I got two new clients. One was a long-term project, and the other was a short-term project. My processes were working like clockwork. My Etsy sales improved by multiple folds. I was starting to gain engagement on my social media platforms as well.

Everything was looking up.

I really think that by applying The 6 Month Rule, I was able to continue this journey. Even if I had decided to quit after the six-month period, I would have done it with no regrets. Giving myself that time to emotionally detach from my business helped me look at everything objectively. This was a life-changing decision, and I'm so glad I made it.

If you'd like to implement the 6 Month Rule for yourself, here's how you can go about it:

Step 1: List out all the reasons why you wish to quit now. *(It doesn't have to be quitting this entrepreneurial journey. It could be removing a product from your mix or a system/process in your business, etc.)*

Step 2: Of all the reasons, take a look at what you can fix or improve in the next six months. Those will be your tasks for the 6 Month period.

Step 3: Identify actionable steps for each item in Step 2. These can be systems or processes you'd like to add to better the structure of your business.

Step 4: Work towards every task on your list. Don't worry about the outcome; just focus on the task at hand.

Step 5: Keep a date set six months down the line. That will be the date you reevaluate your decision to quit.

Step 6: Remember that the clock resets if you've paused in between. That means you have to start the six months again, and you cannot make a decision until you've completed your entire six months. *(If you don't like this rule, you can take it up with my mom, haha!)*

Step 7: At the end of your six months, take some time to evaluate your current standing.

Ask yourself the following questions and make your decision:

◆ When I look back at the list of reasons for quitting six months earlier, how many of them still exist now?

◆ How do I feel about those remaining reasons? Do I think I can eliminate them over time, or will those reasons stay for good?

♦ Am I feeling different about the changes I've made so far?

♦ From where I am now, how do I feel about the future of my business?

♦ What's my final verdict?

It's not that the six months will give you the results you want.

Remember, the 6 Month Rule is about you being neutral, which also means no expectations. I didn't get any clients by the sixth month, but I decided to continue. The six-month time wasn't about getting a client, but it was about understanding my next steps.

And that's what the six-month time does—it gives you clarity.

I'm sure that on this journey, that is not going to be the last time when I contemplate whether I should quit or not. I think that part of this entrepreneurial journey is us making a choice every single day to continue doing what we do.

Sometimes, it gets to a point where we are no longer sure if we want to continue or not. At that moment, we feel we need to make an immediate decision. Given how emotionally invested we are, it can be hard to make the right decision in that moment. Giving ourselves that six-month time allows us to make the healthiest choice.

In or out, shouldn't we give ourselves the time to make sure it is a choice we will not regret later on?

Visit www.themarketingnomad.co/zero-to-four-figures to get access to a printable workbook to help you implement the 6 Month rule.

8.3

Give yourself a "feel bad" time.

I mentioned giving myself a "feel bad" time at the beginning of this book.

I wanted to write more about what a "feel bad" time is and how you can use it. I've been implementing this since my engineering days. Whether it was heartbreak or bad grades, I kept a time limit on how long I allowed myself to feel bad about the situation.

I found that it worked really well because it gave me enough time to process my emotions, and at the same time, it didn't allow me to go into self-pity mode.

In this section, I'll teach you how to give yourself a "feel bad" time that works for you.

Step 1: How long does it take you to process?

The first step is to look at your previous experiences in similar situations and analyze how long it takes you to process your emotions. It's important to know that you will take different amounts of time for different situations.

For example, maybe someone you knew for a few weeks ghosted you, and you're feeling bad. The time you need to process this will differ from the time you need to process if you end a three-year relationship.

For me, it started out with trial and error. I was over-zealous when I started implementing the "feel bad" time. I remember giving myself a "feel bad" time of one day for a significant heartbreak; naturally, it wasn't enough. I had to extend my "feel bad" time.

Years later, I was over-zealous when it came to my business too. I felt silly for feeling bad about something related to my business, and I wanted to get over feeling bad as quickly as possible. So, I gave myself a very short "feel bad" time and expected to get over it by then.

However, it doesn't work that way. We each process things differently, and it is okay to take the time we need, to work through our emotions.

That's why I can't give you a definite answer to this. There have been times when my "feel bad" time was twelve hours. There have also been times when my "feel bad" time was a week.

So, when choosing your "feel bad" time, don't hesitate to give yourself more time even though you want to get over your current feelings quickly. It takes time to process your emotions.

Remember, the point of the "feel bad" time is not to rush through your processing time but to make sure you get out before you start to wallow in self-pity.

Step 2: Use the time to process your emotions.

So, during the "feel bad" time, it's not all fun and games. You're giving yourself this time to work through your emotions. There are different ways to process one's emotions, and I'm neither a psychologist nor a therapist, so I can't recommend any method. All I can say is to find a way that works for you, and if seeking help is one of those methods, then go for it!

I personally journal a lot during my "feel bad" times. I write everything that runs through my mind. I identify the root of why I feel the way I'm feeling.

If I'm frustrated, I write down why I'm feeling that way and what led to me feeling that way. If I'm sad, I recount what has happened and the underlying reason.

Let me give you an example:

One of my launches didn't work out the way I had hoped. I think it was my third or fourth launch, and I was sad about it.

Of course, the surface-level reason for my feeling terrible was that the launch didn't perform as expected. But the underlying cause was that the money from this launch was meant to go into my savings to publish my book someday. Given that the launch made no sales, there was a delay in my plan to save for my book. At this point, I was feeling helpless, and I felt that if things kept going this way, I probably would never be able to save enough. What seemed like me feeling bad for a launch turned out to be me feeling bad that I was falling behind on my timeline for my book launch.

So, it's essential to go to the underlying cause of why you are feeling the way you do. For me, journaling helps me clear my thoughts and enables me to dig deeper. For you, it could be meditation or talking to your therapist. It's essential to find out what works for you.

Step 3: Adjust your "feel bad" time accordingly.

Sometimes you'll underestimate how long it takes to process something, so you may have to extend your "feel bad" time. As long as you're sure that you're extending it to process your emotions and not for a self-pity party, you're good to go.

On the flip side, sometimes, you will also overestimate how long it would take you to process something, so at a time like this, you would want to cut short your "feel bad" time. This is a tricky one because sometimes you may feel like you're feeling better, but you may not have fully processed what you're feeling.

I recommend sticking out to the entire "feel bad" time unless you are 100%

sure you are okay.

Step 4: Get up and get going.

So once your "feel bad" time is over, I follow a rule: I just have to get up and get going.

Once I take my time to feel bad about a situation and I've processed it, I can't go back into the hole again. This means that after I finish my "feel bad" time for something, I've got to dust it off and focus on other aspects of my life. No more feeling bad about it. That's the point of the "feel bad" time.

Yes, sometimes the issues are ongoing or huge, or there's something that may trigger you to feel bad again—that's understandable and completely normal. All you have to do is go into your "feel bad" time again and work through it the same way.

The most important thing about the "feel bad" time is letting yourself know that it is okay to feel bad, but once you're done feeling bad, you've got to get up and get going. We've got to come up to the surface for air at some point, right?

8.4

Every success will have something that didn't go right. Don't forget to analyze that.

My seventh product launch was a success.

My first six? One word answer—Nope.

With my first six product launches, I analyzed what went wrong. When something doesn't go the way you hoped, it is natural that you will look into your systems and processes to check out what you should have done instead. You are also likely to spend time identifying how to improve your strategies and techniques for the next time.

But when something exceeds our expectations, we don't take a second glance at the areas we could have done better. When we have success, we only focus on what went right.

So, when my seventh product launch was a success, I did the same too. I reveled at how everything came together. I patted myself on the back and enjoyed revisiting everything I did right.

I don't think there's anything wrong with enjoying one's win. I believe that the hard work you put in should be recognized by yourself. In fact, I think it is essential to take the time and celebrate one's wins.

Given that my first six launches garnered less than five sales in total, I had a routine to write down what went wrong and how I could improve it for the next launch. As a force of habit, I decided to look at what didn't go right in my seventh product launch.

I didn't think I would find anything and felt that could add to my win's satisfaction. As I recapped the entire seventh launch, I realized that there were a few areas that I could have done better.

For example, given that my last six launches did not perform well, I was so focused on making sure I didn't make any of my previous mistakes during the seventh launch that I forgot to plan out what I would do if I *actually* had a successful launch.

My seventh product was a membership program. My launch went smoothly. But I hadn't planned a process to onboard the people who enrolled in my membership program. So, when ten people enrolled in my membership program on the first day, they were confused about their next steps. Enrolling in a membership program was a different experience for them, and I should have provided more information after they enrolled. Given that they were all people who had known me via social media for the past few months, they didn't think negatively about the lack of information when they enrolled.

So, on Day 2 of my launch, I created an automated email sequence that would explain what the membership program would be like, what people could expect, and what their next steps should be. If I had planned it better, I would have created this email sequence before my launch instead.

As I dug deeper into my actions during the launch, I found a few spots that could have done better to make the entire process smoother. I noted all of those down.

Even though the product and product launch were a success, there were still areas I could improve for the next launch. I realized that no success is perfect, and behind every success, there will be a few things that didn't go right, and it's essential to note them.

You can do this by asking yourself these questions:

- ♦ Were there any bumps along the way to hit this success?

- ♦ How could I have made my journey to the end goal smoother?

- ♦ If I could redo this entire process, what would I do differently?

Knowing the areas of improvement doesn't take away from the win. It helps you understand how to keep improving, and doesn't that pave the way for more wins?

8.5

Sustaining success is a skill.

When I hit my first 100 sales on Etsy, I was ecstatic.

I had invested a lot of time in product research, which had paid off. When I created my first Etsy product, making 100 sales seemed crazy. So, when I hit 100 sales on Etsy, it was clear that my effort to bring sales from 0 to 100 was working.

The thing about success is that we think it is an endpoint.

The tip of a challenging journey.

Once I started seeing success, I realized that success is a plateau. Finding success is just the starting point at the top of the plateau. Reaching the starting point doesn't mean your job is done.

You hear many people and companies achieve massive success and then either disappear or fail.

That's because *sustaining that success is a skill.*

Reaching the end of the plateau, aka sustaining that success, requires strategy and effort.

When I hit those 100 sales, I knew I was doing something right. But the next question that came into my mind was, *"Well, how do I keep this going?"*

The strategies I had implemented were good, but they weren't enough to keep me going. I had to add new approaches to ensure I would keep the same sales frequency or increase it if possible.

I created more paths for people to find my Etsy digital shop. I added thank you vouchers for my customers to get a special discount if they wanted to buy another product from my digital shop. I did more intensive product research. I ensured that customer service was my top priority. My sales frequency eventually increased, and I hit more milestones. I was able to sustain the success I found on Etsy. Through this experience, I started recognizing that every other success needed my time and attention to sustain it.

Frankly, I think sustaining success is the hardest part of this journey.

If you'd like to take the time to sustain your success, then here are a few good questions you can ask yourself:

- ♦ How do I sustain this current success long enough to become a stepping-stone for my subsequent success?

- ♦ Are the current systems and processes enough to sustain the success?

- ♦ What additional strategies can I add?

- ♦ What actionable steps can I take to keep the momentum going?

I wish I could tell you that you'll be able to relax once you achieve success, but that's not true. Once you get to where you hoped to be, your next steps should be to keep yourself there until you're ready to move to the next higher goal. If you can't sustain the current success, don't you think it will take longer to reach your subsequent success?

8.6

Take the time to notice and acknowledge your successes.

Like every human, I dream of success.

Of course, when I started, the successes I dreamed about were smaller. For example, hitting my first 500 followers on Instagram or my first 100 on YouTube. Earning my first four-figure month. Making 100 sales on Etsy.

Each of those successes that I had dreamed of seemed significant to me when I was starting out. I imagined how I would react when I hit those successes— Running around the house, with my hands in the air, even doing a fancy jig, when I hit my first four-figure month. I assumed I'd dance my heart out when I hit my first 100 sales on Etsy.

However, something changed when I hit those successes.

When I hit my first 100 subscribers on YouTube, I didn't celebrate like how I thought I would.

Instead, I wondered how I would get to 500 subscribers.

When I hit my first 100 sales on Etsy, it didn't even occur to me to celebrate. I started worrying about how I could sustain that frequency of sales. Instead of enjoying the win, I was strategizing on how to bring my Etsy sales to 200.

When I hit my first four-figure month, I was more tense about the first four-figure project I had taken on. I wondered if I could pull it off or if I was in over my head. The fact that I got my first four-figure project was something I had wished and wished for, but when I saw the signed contract, all I could think about was the strategies I would implement to successfully complete the project.

There have been so many wins that I didn't take notice of. So many successes showed my dreams coming true, but I didn't recognize them when they finally were realized.

During the lull in my business in 2021, one question was eating at me: What had I achieved since I started my journey?

I didn't have an answer. Each time I looked back, I couldn't see my wins. Not because they weren't there but because I had failed to acknowledge them.

I felt really dejected. Was there really nothing to show for the hard work and effort I had put in?

Since I was already upset about not getting any new clients, it was easy for me to pile on new things to be sad about.

I wondered if this was how my entrepreneurial journey was meant to be. You know, slog, slog, then slog some more, only to feel happy at the endpoint?

I mean, what even was the endpoint? I had absolutely no idea. I was literally creating new milestones for myself as I went along.

Wait a minute, I thought to myself; creating milestones as I went along meant there were previous milestones that I had achieved.

You can't create new milestones if you've not passed older milestones, right?

I paused to think for a bit.

Then I *really* looked back.

My first YouTube video. My first YouTube video that hit 100 views *(This video reached 4,000 views in 2022)*. My first 500 podcast downloads. My first sale on Etsy. My first affiliate sale from my social media platforms. My first brand partnership.

There were so many milestones that I had overlooked. I never took the time to acknowledge them because I immediately focused on the next milestone. That's why it never felt like I had done anything substantial or achieved anything significant. Because I did not acknowledge these wins, naturally it felt like they never happened.

I knew I had to change the way I looked at my milestones. I recognized the importance of acknowledging my wins and my successes.

Yes, it was essential to plan for the next milestone, but it was equally important for me to acknowledge the milestone I had passed.

I also realized that one of the reasons for my previous burnout was because I felt I was putting in all my efforts with no end in sight. I failed to take the time to recognize the results of my actions. I just whizzed past without noticing them.

I started to become more conscious about my wins and successes. Regardless of how big or small that win was, I began to take the time to celebrate it.

The thing about our goals is that it changes the minute we hit that goal. Our vision moves on to the next goal. As entrepreneurs, we are ambitious.

There's nothing wrong with that.

(Over the years, being ambitious has taken a negative connotation especially for certain races and genders, but over here, in my safe space, we're all ambition-positive. It's a term I'm coining for an ideology that acknowledges and affirms each person's pursuit of their healthy ambition, regardless of

preconceived notions of their race, gender, age, social strata, etc.)

We're always looking at the next step. It's in our nature, and I believe that to be a trait that helps us keep going even though this journey is challenging.

However, in our pursuit of new success, we often forget the previous successes that helped us get to the new success.

If we keep working towards hitting our next goal without acknowledging the last goal that we worked so hard to achieve, then at some point, it will feel like we have nothing to show for the efforts we have put in.

That's an easy spiral into burnout.

I say "we" because this is a lesson I still have to remember all the time. It is not easy for me to recognize my wins. It doesn't come naturally to me to celebrate my little victories along the way. It is a conscious effort for me to intentionally pause and remind myself to feel happy about my current win. I literally have to tell myself to enjoy the feeling of achieving my goal.

But I do this because by acknowledging my wins as I achieve them, no matter how big or small, I show myself the results of my efforts and hard work. I show myself that there are tangible achievements that I have made so far. That helps me believe that there is meaning to my efforts, and it helps me to keep moving forward toward my next goal.

So, take some time today and remember all the wins you have achieved to get to where you are today. Promise yourself to acknowledge your wins and successes from this moment on.

Here are two ways you can go about it, so you never forget to keep a tab of your successes:

Step 1: Grab your weekly task planner.

Step 2: In the notes section, write down three previous week's achievements.

OR

Step 1: Grab an empty box.

Step 2: Each time you have a win, write it on a piece of paper, fold it and drop it into the box.

Step 3: If you're ever feeling low, open the box and read as many chits as you can to make yourself feel better.

The point is, you've got to find a way to keep reminding yourself of your successes. Don't you think you owe this to your past and future self to keep renewing your faith in yourself by celebrating the wins that shaped your path?

8.7

You and only you get to define what success means to you.

This lesson basically summarizes why I'm even writing this book.

Especially in the digital entrepreneurial world, there are so many preconceived notions about what determines success.

I felt this immense pressure when I myself became a digital entrepreneur. For a while, I also believed that I wasn't successful until I had achieved everyone else's idea of success. I was forced to see success only in terms of how everyone defined it.

Success meant five or six-figure launches.

Success meant hitting 100,000 subscribers on YouTube.

Success meant having a seven-figure business.

Was I supposed to wait till I hit these to feel successful?

Was I not allowed to feel successful otherwise?

That sounded ridiculous when I said it out loud. Why was I letting other people control *my* narrative?

Someday I'm going to hit 100,000 subscribers on YouTube. It may take me five years. It may take me ten. Does that mean I'm not going to consider myself a success until then?

That doesn't seem right.

I've heard from countless entrepreneurs who feel like they haven't achieved anything, only because they focus on the narrative set by everyone else.

So much hard work and dedication go into this journey—*our* hard work and *our* dedication. That also means we get to decide what *our* success is.

Once I realized this, I started focusing on the narrative I wanted to have for myself.

What did *I* define as success for myself?

What were *my* milestones?

What did *I* want to achieve?

I could have waited till I hit seven figures to feel that my lessons were worthy enough to share with the world. Frankly, I would never have written this book if I didn't define my successes.

There wouldn't be stories to tell because I would never have viewed anything I've done so far as a success. I got the confidence to write this book because of how *I* defined what success means to me, and for me, having the courage to write this book at the stage of growth I'm in, is a success by itself.

That was enough for me to share my lessons in this book you're reading. I mean come on, I've managed to write about sixty-one, mind you, *six one* lessons within three years of my entrepreneurial journey. Why shouldn't I be proud of it?

Really, it doesn't matter how the book sales go. To me, pushing myself to be vulnerable while writing this book is a success, and one I will celebrate.

Because only I get to define what success means to me.

The same goes for every single success that I have celebrated until now.

Hitting my first three-figure month, then consecutive three-figure months, then my first 100 followers on my social media platforms or making my first fifty sales on Etsy.

These were all successes I defined for myself. If I had let everyone else control the narrative, I would never have recognized all these fantastic milestones I was hitting. I would never have gotten the opportunity to acknowledge that my efforts were paying off.

If there's one thing you can take away from this book, it's that ***you get to control your narrative.***

Only you get to define what success means to you.

No matter how big or small or silly or weird it may seem to anyone else, only you get to point to it and say, *"Yup, that's a success for me!"*

This is your journey, so why shouldn't ***you*** be the one to define what success means to you?

... and I'm just getting started.

YOUR TURN.

This journey has not been easy for me, but it has been one of the best decisions of my life. For me to write an entire book about hitting consistent four-figure months has been liberating, to say the least. This book has helped me make peace with where I am right now and fall in love with the journey.

I started writing this book to bring awareness about the illusion of success that looms in this digital entrepreneurial world. Many times I've been pressured to feel nonchalant about my success because it wasn't perceived as a success by the people around me. There have been times when I've stopped myself from being proud, only because the milestone I hit wasn't a milestone that others looked at in awe.

But that's not right.

The truth is that you get to define your success. You absolutely get to choose which ones you want to celebrate. No win is too small, and every kind of success is extraordinary. There is also no right way to define success. What success means to you may not be what others perceive as success, and that's okay.

If I could write an entire 81,000-word book with sixty-one lessons I have learned from *Zero to Four Figures*, I hope I've conveyed that every figure counts. Every figure you hit in this journey matters. You don't have to wait until you hit seven figures to be proud of how far you've come. You can start being proud from the minute you begin this journey.

Yes, in this digital entrepreneurial world, there is a lot of emphasis on hitting six or seven figures to recognize someone's success, but it is time for us to change the narrative. It is time for us to be proud of wherever we are at.

Consistent two-figure months?

First three-figure month?

Consistent three-figure months?

First four-figure month?

Consistent four-figure months?

First five-figure project?

Regardless of where you are, it is a success worthy of announcing to the world. If there's anything you take away from the book, I would like it to be this:

Take the time today to acknowledge where you are at. Look back at how far you've come and look at your journey objectively. See every win for what it is—worthy of celebration!

The longer we wait to share our wins, however big or small they may seem, the longer it takes for us to feel that we are heading in the right direction. It's harder to have faith in the more challenging times when you don't take the time to acknowledge how far you've come and the milestones you've successfully crossed.

Not just that, the more each of us starts getting comfortable with talking about where we are, the easier it becomes for us to feel encouraged about our journey. I hope my book inspires you to define your successes and celebrate the wins you are proud of. It doesn't matter how other people perceive that win, as long as *you* perceive it as a win.

Every journey is different, and we must learn to embrace every unique win.

We get to choose our narrative of what success means to us.

After all, hopping on this digital entrepreneurship journey is no ordinary feat, and the first person who must recognize that is ourselves.

So, take some time today, and hop along with me on the Zero to Four Figures Challenge [#zerotofourfigures]:

Step 1: Grab your phone.

Step 2: Look at yourself in the mirror. You can choose to hold my book up. Don't forget to smile. ☺

Step 3: Click a picture and on the picture, share one win that you defined as a success for yourself!

Step 4: You can repeat this as many times as you'd like. With every new figure you hit, or every new success that you define for yourself, you can hop on the challenge again.

Step 5: Don't forget to tag me [@themarketingnomad] as I would love to be a part of your success and cheer you on! You can use the hashtag [#zerotofourfigures] which will allow you to connect with like-minded entrepreneurs in our Zero to Four Figures community.

Can't wait to see all your successes! ☺

Before I sign off, I would like to request something from you: If this book has helped you in any way, *please consider leaving a review on Amazon and/or Goodreads.* This is the best way you can help me help more entrepreneurs and business owners like you. Here's a QR code for the review links (or you can visit themarketingnomad.co/ztff-review).

Don't forget to share this book with your other entrepreneur friends!

It's on us to change the narrative of our own entrepreneurial journey, and the more entrepreneurs and business owners are aware of this, the easier it becomes to create a healthier environment for all of us. We all want that, don't we?

Also, don't forget to grab your workbooks at _www.themarketingnomad.co/zero-to-four-figures_. You'll also receive regular newsletters from me so we can continue redefining success together!

ACKNOWLEDGEMENTS

This book wouldn't be in your hands without the help and support of so many incredible people. I want to take the time to acknowledge the people who have been a part of my journey and who have helped me bring this book to life.

Starting off with my parents. Ma, Pa, thank you for always taking the time to teach me all the lessons that eventually helped me lead the life I have always dreamed of. You've shaped how I show up today, and I will always be grateful for that.

Then comes my little sister, Pinky. My life. Words cannot express how much I love you. I'm so grateful and proud to be your sister. Thank you for always having my back and encouraging me to do what my heart desired. My forever partner-in-crime.

Mr. BRV Murthy and Mrs. Usha Murthy (aka "Barbie" uncle and aunty), thank you for always watching over me and my family. Regardless of where I am in the world, I've always felt your blessing. When I told you about my entrepreneurial journey, you said you were proud of me for doing something different, and you encouraged me to keep pursuing my passion. You have no idea how much I needed to hear that at the time. Thank you for everything you have selflessly done for my family.

Mr. Chuck Schwartz, my mentor, thank you for your unwavering support since we met. You've been there for me during my lows and cheered me for my wins. Thank you for taking me under your wing and mentoring me through this crazy roller coaster. I'm so thankful you are a part of my entrepreneurial journey.

Ashu, Manu mama, and Sumatte, thank you for helping me when I first landed in America. It was a new phase of my life, and I definitely needed help adjusting. Ashu, you called me every single weekend just to check in with me while I was doing my MBA, and you were always making sure I was happy. I miss you more with each passing day. I remember your thoughts on my blog posts and how much you loved my writing. I know you would have been proud of this book. Manu mama, thank you for being there by my side when I was leaving America. I'm not the best at asking for help, but I'm so grateful you were always there to offer it.

To my darling dog, Dollar. You were my source of strength during the worst times of my life, and I will always cherish the ten years of unconditional love you brought us. We are so blessed you stepped into our lives. Miss you, my cutchie boy.

A girl is nothing without her best friends, and I have to thank mine.

Annie Janofsky, you beautiful soul, you. Thank you for always being there for me. You've been there for the 3 a.m. frantic calls and crazy 3 p.m. calls. You're such a bright light, a powerful human, and I'm thankful you are a part of my journey.

Sahithi Tulluru, you are such an inspiration to me, and I look up to you. We've been through some rough times together, and I'm so proud of how far we've come. You've had my back since day one, and I will be forever grateful for that.

My journey to where I am today started from Primary 3. I have to thank my Primary 3 teacher, Ms. Rae Wong (White Sands Primary School, 2001). I cannot express how powerful an impact you have left in my life. I was a handful at that age, and somehow you taught me how to channel my mind and energy into being the best version of myself. You recognized my strengths and always reminded me to grow them. You saw something in me that I didn't. Knowing that someone believed in me when I was only nine years old really motivated me to push through the rough times *(still motivates me even to this day),* and I have you to thank for that.

I would also like to thank a few more teachers who always encouraged me to be a better version of myself:

Ms. Nadia (Yishun Primary School, Singapore, 1999), I remember writing a picture composition, and you asked me to read it in front of the class. Thank you for taking the time to show me I had a talent for writing. That was the first time I knew I was going to be an author someday. I look back at that memory fondly, and this book is the start of me actualizing that dream.

Thank you for recognizing my writing talent, Mr. Bernard Fernando (White Sands Primary School, Singapore, 2003). Your evaluations of my composition book made me confident in my writing. I remember half-heartedly writing a composition once, and you commented that you expected better from me as you knew I had it in me to write from my heart. From that day on, I have always written from my heart and soul, and I have you to thank for that.

I have to thank my teachers at The Brigade School, Bangalore (2004 – 2011):

Mrs. Shalini Jagdish, thank you for being patient with me as I learned how to express myself. You always encouraged me to shine my light, regardless of what anyone else thought, and that lesson will always stay with me.

Mrs. Jyothi Srinath, thank you for recognizing my love for writing and holding my writing to higher standards. You saw my potential, and you always reminded me to keep getting better at it. You would make me read my answers in front of the class because you thought they were good, and it was in those tiny moments that my confidence in writing really grew.

Mrs. Nandini Yogesh, you are so full of life. You always knew I would make a difference to the people around me, and you never failed to remind me to recognize my power. Thank you for always believing in me.

Then we come to my engineering teachers, PES—Bangalore South Campus (2011 – 2016)

Mr. Subhash Kulkarni, thank you for always making me comfortable enough to ask for help during my low moments. You taught me to take my failures in stride and rise above them. That is a lesson I have carried forward in my life, whether for my personal life or even my business.

Mr. Prashanth Reddy, thank you for always letting me know it was okay to be different. You knew I was destined for something bigger, and you always encouraged me to follow my heart.

Mr. Nagendra Prasad, thank you for helping me recognize that I had my own strengths, and it was okay if they weren't the strengths of people around me. You always encouraged me to focus on my strengths, which led me to find my career path.

Mr. Anand VM, you cared about me and my well-being. You believed I was meant to do more with my life, even when I couldn't believe it myself. You saw me for my strengths and never judged me even though I was different. Your kindness towards me during my engineering days made me stronger. For that, I will always be grateful to you.

Mrs. Prafulla, you are an absolute gem. You went above and beyond to help me during my lowest moments. You took the time to listen to me when I was struggling. You also took extra classes just for me to better prepare for the exams. You helped me believe in myself again. I struggled to find my passion at the time, and you always told me everything would soon be okay. Thank you for everything.

Mr. Murlidhar S., thank you for recognizing when something was wrong with me during my engineering days. I hadn't realized it until you brought it to my attention, and I will always be grateful to you. In that moment of speaking with you, I realized my life was no longer in control. After that day, I gained some semblance of control over my life. If you hadn't cared to ask me what was wrong, I know my life would have looked very different today. I wouldn't have worked harder to get into an MBA program if it wasn't for our conversation that day. Thank you.

Then we come to my professors at Rochester Institute of Technology (2016-2018):

Ms. Laurie Dwyer, you have always been my inspiration. It was in your marketing class that I decided I would pursue my career in Marketing. Thank you for always taking the time to answer all my questions and doubts and encouraging me to be a better marketer. I have learned so much from you and will always be grateful.

Mr. Zhi Tang, thank you for recognizing my potential and bringing some of my strengths to my attention. You were always keen to hear my thoughts and opinions. You went above and beyond to teach the practical side of business, and I successfully applied the lessons you taught when I started my entrepreneurial journey.

Now I'd like to thank the people who were part of my time at EmPower Solar, New York (2018 – 2019):

Mr. David G. Schieren (CEO), thank you for being an inspiration to me. Your passion and dedication in making a difference to the people around you inspire me as a business owner to keep going. Even today, I remember how you handled the lows and how positive you always were, regardless of the odds against you. Each time I hit a low in my business, I've taken inspiration from you and kept going. The life and business lessons you've taught me are priceless, and I am grateful for that.

Mrs. Tara McDermott (Marketing Manager, 2018, Director of Stakeholder Relations, 2022), thank you, thank you, thank you. I cannot even begin to express how much I learned from you in the one year I worked under you. You were a fantastic mentor who always encouraged me to grow. From the first interview with EmPower Solar, you knew I would be a CEO someday, and that has motivated me so much during my entrepreneurial journey. Everything you taught me provided a good starting point for me as a marketing strategy consultant, and for that, I am grateful. Thank you for being my mentor, an amazing colleague, and my friend during my time at

EmPower Solar.

Mr. Zack Lerman and Mr. Mike Kafka, you guys are extraordinary. Thank you for patiently teaching me sales, even though I was a marketer. You always took the time to make sure I understood the concepts. Those have helped me as a business owner/digital entrepreneur, and I thank you.

Seneca, Summer, and Anjalu, my fabulous colleagues and friends! You were there for me every step. Thank you for helping me through one of the lowest points of my life and cheering me on as I started my entrepreneurial journey. I will always be grateful for that.

To the entire team at EmPower Solar, I miss you guys so much. You made every single day of my time at EmPower Solar so memorable, and I learned a lot about life and sales from you. Each one of you extended your help and support to me when I was leaving, and I will always remember it. Thank you.

Now I'd like to thank the people who have helped me bring this book to life.

To my editor, Sierra Cotton, for doing a phenomenal job with the editing. Thank you for patiently answering every panicked question I had and making sure this book would be the best version of itself.

To my beta readers, Kenneth Reid, Michael Camarillo, Folasade Taiwo, Meghana Sridhar, Jaskirat Singh, Amogh Jeerige, Andrea Chomiczuk, Elsie Baker and Pooja Raju, words cannot express how grateful I am to have your help. Each one of you patiently read my words, gave honest feedback, and transformed this book into what it is today. You also encouraged me to keep going and your continued support for me and my entrepreneurial journey has touched my heart.

To all my followers, subscribers, listeners, and friends I've made along the way, thank you for always giving me a safe space to be myself, and to voice my thoughts. The amount of love you have given me in the last three years has been beyond my wildest dreams and I'm grateful you are on this roller coaster ride with me!

The only question that remains is, where are we headed to next? *wink*

Last but not the least, my dear reader. You are the reason I even wrote this book. Thank you for picking this book and taking the time to read about my journey and my lessons learned so far. I want you to know that you are amazing, and you are absolutely worthy of defining your own success. I'm right here beside you, cheering you on! Don't ever forget that!

Lots of love,
Prithvi Madhukar, aka The Marketing Nomad

Prithvi Madhukar—aka The Marketing Nomad—is a quirky digital entrepreneur and business owner with a passion for marketing and a zest for life. She is a Podcaster (Top 100 in Marketing—India, Top 10% Global), YouTuber, Etsy Shop Owner, Author, Skillshare Teacher, and Influencer. She is also the CEO of The Marketing Nomad LLC, a global Marketing Consultancy Firm in Delaware that has helped sixty-plus clients from eight different countries as of 2022. As a location-independent Marketing Strategy Consultant, she empowers business owners to confidently implement long-term marketing strategies to grow the business they love. She enjoys Bollywood dancing in her free time.

Prithvi's life story is pretty interesting. She completed her engineering degree only to realize her passion for marketing. After choosing to follow her passion and completing her MBA with a concentration in Marketing, she worked at a top solar firm in New York for a year. When her H-1B work visa was not processed, she was forced to leave the US, which meant she had to leave her fantastic full-time job, amazing colleagues, best friends, and a place she had called home for three years.

Absolutely devastated and desperate to find hope in life again, she decided to risk her entire savings and invest in her dream of becoming a digital entrepreneur in 2019. After successfully finding ways to navigate through her journey, she made it her mission to empower other digital entrepreneurs and business owners with marketing, business, and mindset help to grow the business they love. Her content on all platforms be it her book or her videos, share a genuine and authentic insight into her personal and professional life. It has inspired many to continue pursuing their own entrepreneurial journeys.

As she continues to dive deeper into the entrepreneurial world, she invites you to join her roller coaster ride. If you'd like to know more about her marketing strategy consultation services or catch her on all her social media platforms, you can use this QR code, or you can visit themarketingnomad.co/main

PLATFORMS

Website:
themarketingnomad.co

Instagram:
@themarketingnomad

Twitter:
@themrktgnomad

YouTube:
youtube.com/c/themarketingnomad

Podcast:
The Marketing Nomad Show
(Available on Apple Podcasts, Spotify, Google Podcasts, Amazon Music, iHeartRadio, Stitcher, and all major podcast platforms)

LinkedIn:
linkedin.com/in/prithvimadhukar/

Etsy Digital Shop
etsy.com/shop/themarketingnomadco

Skillshare:
skillshare.com/user/themarketingnomad